MW00948698

FROM CONFLICT TO CLOSENESS - THE COUPLES THERAPY PLAYBOOK

Overcome Emotional Distance, Rebuild Trust, and
Improve Communication for Lasting Satisfaction and
Joy in Your Relationship

THOMAS R. BÄCHLER

Book Cover by Thomas Bächler

Illustrations by Thomas Bächler

1st edition 2024

Contents

Introduction

Did you know that over 65% of relationship breakdowns are attributed to poor communication? If you find yourself nodding along or perhaps even feeling a sting of recognition, you're not alone. Many couples struggle silently with emotional distance, the erosion of trust, and difficult conversations, not realizing that the heart of the issue often lies in how they communicate.

This workbook is designed as both a journey and a toolkit to bridge these gaps. It's designed to guide you and your partner through the intricate dance of understanding, appreciating, and connecting with each other on a deeper level. Think of it as a map, charting the course to a relationship marked by enhanced trust, clearer communication, and a renewed sense of closeness.

My own journey into the realm of couples therapy began not in a professional setting but within the walls of my own home. As a father and husband, I've navigated the choppy waters of relationship challenges. These experiences have not only humbled me but have ignited a passion to share what I've learned with others. I've seen firsthand how easy it is to feel disconnected and how rewarding the path to reconnection can be. This workbook stems from a blend of personal trials and professional research aimed at delivering practical and scientifically-backed strategies to strengthen your relationship.

The vision behind this book is simple yet profound: to equip you with the tools necessary to transform your relationship dynamics. Through carefully crafted exercises, thoughtful questions, and actionable strategies, this workbook is structured to provide significant benefits that are both immediate and long-lasting. Whether you're looking to revitalize a weary relationship or deepen an already strong connection, the guidance offered here is intended to be universally applicable and deeply transformative.

With scientific research integrated into practical application, this workbook not only tells you what works but also shows you how to apply these strategies in your everyday life. Each chapter builds on the last, creating a comprehensive guide that addresses various aspects of relationship dynamics, from managing conflicts to enhancing intimacy.

By the end of this journey, I hope you will have acquired not just improved communication skills but also a deeper emotional connection with your partner, bringing more joy and satisfaction into your relationship. This workbook is designed to encourage you at every step as you work towards a more fulfilling partnership.

In closing, I want to reassure you that you are not navigating your struggles alone. This workbook represents a step towards understanding your partner better and also building a lasting bond based on mutual respect and love. Together, let's turn the challenges into stepping stones for a stronger relationship.

Welcome to a new chapter in your journey together. Let's make it a beautiful one.

ONE

Laying the Foundations of Effective Communication

H ave you ever felt misunderstood by your partner or perhaps found yourself confused by their perspective? Words often fall short or get tangled in the web of emotions during difficult conversations. This first chapter is dedicated to dismantling those barriers through effective communication, starting with the cornerstone of all successful interactions: active listening. We often think we're listening, but more often than not, we're focused on what we want to say next, caught up in our thoughts, which makes genuine understanding elusive. Here, we'll explore how to truly listen—not just to the words but to the whole message being conveyed, setting the stage for deeper connection and understanding.

1.1 The Art of Active Listening

Active listening is about so much more than hearing words; it's an active process where you make a conscious effort to understand the complete message being conveyed by your partner. This includes unspoken elements like tone of voice and body language, as well as the emotional undertones woven through their words. Imagine a scenario where your partner is sharing how overwhelmed they feel. They say they're "fine," yet their voice is flat, and their eyes are downcast. Active listening allows you to detect these discrepancies between words and non-verbal cues, offering a chance to dig deeper and offer support to address their true feelings.

To become an adept active listener, start with these foundational steps:

1. **MAINTAIN EYE CONTACT:** This shows your partner that you are fully engaged and value what they are saying.
2. **NOD AND OFFER VERBAL AFFIRMATIONS:** Simple cues like nodding your head or saying "I see" or "Go on" reassure your partner that you are involved in the conversation.
3. **AVOID INTERRUPTING:** Let them finish their thoughts without jumping in with your solutions or opinions. This can be challenging, especially if you think you have the perfect advice, but patience here is crucial.
4. **REFLECT FEELINGS:** After they've finished speaking, reflect back on what you've heard, both content and emotions. For example, "It sounds like you're really stretched thin at work, and it's making you feel stressed."

Despite our best intentions, several barriers can impede effective listening. One of the most common is the habit of formulating your response while the other person is still speaking. This detracts you from genuinely understanding them and also makes your partner feel unheard. Personal biases, past experiences, and our own emotional response can also cloud our interpretation of what's being shared, affecting our interpretation and understanding. Recognizing these barriers is the first step toward mitigating them, paving the way for clearer, more empathetic exchanges.

To enhance your listening skills, consider these exercises:

- **REPEAT BACK:** After your partner shares something with you, repeat back in your own words what you understood. Ask them to confirm if you've got it right. This improves your listening skills and helps immediately clarify any miscommunications.
- **LISTENING DRILLS:** Set aside time with your partner where you talk about a neutral topic for a few minutes. The listener should focus solely on the speaker's words, tone, and body language without planning any response. After the session, the listener recounts everything they picked up, including any inferred emotional states.

Interactive Exercise: Reflective Listening Journal

To deepen your understanding of active listening:

1 Maintain a reflective listening journal for a week.

2 After each significant conversation with your partner, jot down key points you picked up, including words, tone, and body language.

3 Reflect on how these elements either clarified or obscured the message. This exercise will enhance your awareness of how much information you're actually absorbing and what might be slipping through the cracks.

By dedicating yourself to improving your active listening skills, you're not just enhancing communication with your partner; you're also opening doors to a more empathetic, connected, and understanding relationship.

1.2 Expressing Needs Without Conflict

Understanding and effectively communicating our personal needs can often be the bridge between sustained misunderstandings and harmonious coexistence in a relationship. Before you can share these needs with your partner, self-reflect to pinpoint precisely what you require from your relationship. This isn't about the superficial day-to-day desires but rather the deeper emotional, physical, and intellectual needs that foster a sense of fulfillment and security. For instance, consider the difference between needing more help around the house versus needing your partner to understand why a clean and orderly home environment is crucial to your peace of mind. Identifying the root of your needs often clarifies what might initially seem like a simple preference or annoyance.

To embark on this self-reflection, ask yourself what makes you feel most valued and loved in your relationship. Is it when your partner actively listens to you and supports your career moves? Or perhaps when they spend quality time with you without distractions? Writing down instances when you felt particularly happy or disappointed can help you discover patterns that point directly to your core needs. Tools like journaling or meditation can facilitate this introspection, giving you a clearer picture of what to communicate to your partner.

Once your needs are clear, expressing them in a way that is constructive and non-confrontational is vital. This is where the power of "I" statements comes into play. Instead of saying, "You never help around the house," which can lead to defensiveness, try, "I feel supported when we share household responsibilities." This slight shift in phrasing can make a significant difference in how your message is received. It moves the conversation from a blame game to an expression of your feelings and needs, making it easier for your partner to hear and understand where you're coming from without feeling attacked.

The setting in which you choose to discuss your needs also plays a crucial role in how the conversation unfolds. Timing and environment can heavily influence the outcome of your discussion. It's generally best to choose a moment when both you and your partner are calm and not distracted by external stressors like work or childcare. A quiet, private setting, free from the hustle and bustle of daily life, also helps create a space where both partners can be more open and receptive. Sometimes, when things in life are so busy, it can be difficult to find a quiet, calm time. Another option that works well is to ask if your partner can identify a time later for the conversation. Or, if the conversation needs to happen in the moment (from the perspective of the person who needs to share), asking, "Do you have the emotional space for a conversation about this right now?" can be really helpful.

Incorporating role-playing exercises can further enhance your ability to express needs constructively. By creating scenarios in which you and your partner practice expressing and responding to needs in a controlled environment, you can develop and refine effective communication skills. These exercises help you rehearse what you want to say and, in anticipating potential responses from your partner, allow you to emotionally and mentally prepare for the actual conversation. One useful approach is to take turns expressing a need and then discussing as a couple how the message could be improved. This enhances understanding and builds a supportive environment for open communication.

Role-playing and rehearsing are not about scripting your relationship interactions to the letter but rather about gaining confidence and fluency in expressing your genuine feelings and needs. As you both practice and become more comfortable with this form of communication, you'll find that it becomes easier to address issues as they arise, reducing conflict and enhancing the overall quality of your relationship. Through these methods, coupled with a commitment to understanding and meeting each other's needs, you create a dynamic where both partners feel valued, understood, respected, and deeply connected.

1.3 Non-Verbal Communication Cues

The unspoken dialogue that occurs in every interaction we have is often more telling than the words we exchange. Non-verbal communication, including our facial expressions, gestures, and posture, plays an indispensable role in the way we convey and interpret messages. Think about a time when a simple smile from your partner lightened a tense moment, or consider how a defensive arm-cross might have escalated a disagreement. These non-verbal cues can either enrich or undermine the verbal messages we convey, acting as silent orchestrators of the emotional tone of our dialogues.

Understanding and mastering the subtleties of body language can significantly enhance the quality of our interactions. Positive body language, such as nodding affirmatively, leaning slightly forward, or maintaining an open posture, can affirm our engagement and receptiveness to our partner's concerns. It reassures them that we are present and invested in the conversation, fostering a supportive environment. Conversely, negative body language—like avoiding eye contact, frowning, or closed-off postures—can signal disinterest, disagreement, or even disdain, which can shut down open communication and deepen emotional distances.

The skill of reading your partner's non-verbal cues is just as crucial as being mindful of your own. It involves paying close attention to the inconspicuous yet revealing signals that indicate their feelings and reactions. For instance, if, during a discussion, your partner continually taps their foot or fidgets, they might be experiencing anxiety or impatience. Recognizing these signs gives you a cue to adjust the course of the conversation or address their discomfort directly, perhaps by asking what's really on their mind or if there's something they would like to talk about more urgently.

Aligning your verbal and non-verbal communication is essential to avoid sending mixed or confusing signals. Imagine telling your partner you're happy to discuss something, yet your arms are crossed, and your brow is furrowed. The mixed signals make it difficult for your partner to feel secure in the conversation, likely leading to misunderstandings or conflict. And, if the topic is a sensitive one, the partner speaking may feel uncomfortable discussing the core issue, and they may deflect to something more surface level, thus removing the opportunity to discuss what is actually causing the problem.

Your body language needs to echo the sentiments and messages you're sharing verbally, creating coherence in your communication that reinforces trust and clarity.

To improve your non-verbal communication, engage in exercises that focus on mirroring and matching body language. This could involve sitting face to face and mimicking each other's postures and gestures. This exercise helps build empathy and makes you more aware of how body language can influence perception and feelings. Additionally, playing games like charades can be an enjoyable way to become more attuned to interpreting each other's physical expressions. Such activities encourage you to pay closer attention to how much can be communicated without words and develop a sharper instinct for reading the room—skills that are invaluable in any relationship.

These practices aren't just about improving how you communicate; they're about deepening your connection with your partner by ensuring you're both heard and understood, not just through the words you speak but through the silent language of your bodies. As you become more attuned to the nuances of this silent language, your ability to navigate and enrich your relationship will strengthen day by day.

1.4 The Role of Tone and Timing in Difficult Conversations

The tone of voice you adopt and the timing of your conversations can play pivotal roles in the outcome of your communications, especially during sensitive or potentially heated discussions. Think about how a simple statement like "We need to talk" can feel like an ominous prelude depending on how it's said—either calmly and invitingly or sharply and urgently. Tone can convey empathy, aggression, indifference, or love, thus shaping the emotional climate of a dialogue before the content even comes into play. For instance, a soft, gentle tone can help soothe and defuse a potentially volatile exchange. It invites openness and vulnerability, making it easier for both partners to express their feelings without fear of judgment or escalation. On the other hand, a harsh, loud tone might do just the opposite, putting the listener on the defensive and escalating the conflict before the real issues are even addressed.

The significance of timing cannot be overstated either. Engaging in a serious conversation when one partner is already stressed or distracted can lead to misunderstandings and resentment. The right moment for a challenging discussion is when both partners are relatively calm and have the mental and emotional bandwidth to deal with the topic at hand. This doesn't mean waiting for a perfect moment—because, let's be honest, perfect moments are rare—but rather, choosing a time when both of you are least likely to be overwhelmed by external pressures. This could be after dinner, during a quiet evening at home, or perhaps during a leisurely weekend morning when you're both more relaxed and receptive. If the conversation needs to happen right away, you could also ask the person who needs to share, "Do you have the emotional space for a conversation about this right now?"

Managing your tone during conversations requires mindfulness and self-control, particularly in heated moments. One effective technique is to consciously slow down your speech and lower the volume of your voice. This deliberate modulation can have a calming effect on both you and your partner. Additionally, incorporating pauses into your speech allows you to collect your thoughts and gives your partner space to process the information, reducing the chances of reactive responses. Breathing exercises can also be incredibly helpful in managing your tone. Taking a deep breath before you respond gives you a moment to calm your nervous system and choose your words and tone more carefully, ensuring that your emotions don't override the message you intend to convey.

Role-playing different scenarios with varying tones and timings can be an enlightening exercise for couples. It allows you to explore how different approaches affect the dynamics of a conversation. For instance, you might take turns discussing a common issue using different tones and at different times of the day to observe how these variables influence the interaction. This not only helps in understanding the impact of tone and timing but also prepares you for real-life conversations, providing a safer, structured environment to experiment and learn.

Through conscious practice and attention to these aspects of communication, you can significantly enhance the quality and effectiveness of your interactions. Remember, *how* and *when* you convey your message can turn the tide of a conversation from conflict to collaboration.

TWO

Deepening Emotional Connection

Have you ever wondered why some couples seem to effortlessly understand each other while others struggle to connect on an emotional level? It's not just about love or attraction—emotional intelligence plays a crucial role in fostering a deep and lasting connection. Emotional intelligence, or EI, is the ability to recognize, understand, and manage our own emotions, as well as the emotions of others. It's what helps us navigate the complexities of our relationships with empathy and insight. In this chapter, we'll delve into the components of EI and explore how enhancing it can transform your relationship.

2.1 Building Emotional Intelligence in Relationships

Understanding emotional intelligence begins with acknowledging its five key components:

- Self-awareness
- Self-regulation
- Motivation
- Empathy
- Social skills

SELF-AWARENESS involves recognizing your own emotions and how they affect your thoughts and behaviors. Imagine a scenario where you feel irritated because your partner forgot an important date. Instead of immediately reacting with anger, self-awareness allows you to pause and identify the underlying emotion, whether it's feeling unappreciated or overlooked. This pause can make all the difference in how you choose to address the situation.

SELF-REGULATION is the ability to manage your emotions and impulses, maintaining control even in stressful situations. It's about responding thoughtfully rather than reacting impulsively. For instance, when a disagreement arises, instead of shouting or shutting down, self-regulation helps you take a deep breath and respond calmly. And if you feel that you might shut down, self-regulation allows you to be aware of that and communicate to your partner that you need a few minutes of space, because otherwise you might not be fully present and able to give the conversation the attention it deserves.

MOTIVATION in EI refers to the inner drive to achieve goals and maintain a positive attitude despite setbacks. In relationships, this means being committed to working through challenges and staying focused on building a strong partnership.

EMPATHY is the ability to understand and share the feelings of others. It's not just about recognizing your partner's emotions but feeling them as if they were your own. This can lead to deeper connections and more meaningful interactions.

SOCIAL SKILLS involve managing relationships to move them in the desired direction, whether it's resolving conflicts, building rapport, or inspiring others. In a relationship, strong social skills mean effective communication and the ability to work collaboratively towards common goals.

Assessing you and your partner's emotional intelligence can provide valuable insights into your relationship dynamics. Start with self-evaluations and observations of how you handle emotional situations. Consider keeping a journal where you note your reactions to various emotional triggers and reflect on whether your responses align with the principles of EI. For example, after a heated argument, write down what triggered your emotional response, how you reacted, and how you could have handled it differently. Observing your partner's reactions in similar situations can also offer clues about their EI.

Improving EI is a continuous process that involves intentional practice and reflection. For self-awareness, mindfulness practices such as meditation or regular self-reflection can help you become more attuned to your emotions. Breathing techniques are excellent for self-regulation, helping you stay calm and composed in stressful moments. Setting shared goals with your partner can boost motivation, creating a sense of purpose and direction in your relationship. Practice empathy by actively listening to your partner without judgment, validating their feelings, and expressing understanding. Finally, enhance your social skills by working on effective communication, conflict resolution, and teamwork.

The impact of enhanced EI on relationships is profound. Take the case of Maya and Alex, who struggled with constant misunderstandings and emotional distance. Through improving their EI, they learned to recognize their own emotional triggers and respond more thoughtfully. Maya became more aware of her tendency to withdraw when stressed, while Alex learned to manage his frustrations more effectively. By practicing empathy, they began to understand and validate each other's feelings, leading to fewer conflicts and a stronger emotional bond.

Reflective Exercise: Emotional Intelligence Self-Assessment

Take a moment to assess your own emotional intelligence. Reflect on recent interactions with your partner and ask yourself the following questions:

- How aware am I of my emotions in these moments?
- How well do I manage my reactions to emotional triggers?
- Do I stay motivated to work through challenges?
- How empathetic am I towards my partner's feelings?
- How effectively do I communicate and resolve conflicts?

Write down your reflections and discuss them with your partner, identifying areas for growth and supporting each other in the journey towards enhanced emotional intelligence.

2.2 The Power of Empathy: Understanding Your Partner's Feelings

Empathy, often described as the ability to put yourself in someone else's shoes, is the cornerstone of any successful relationship. It's what allows you to truly connect with your partner, moving beyond your own perspective to understand and share their emotional experiences. Empathy isn't just one-dimensional; it comprises both cognitive and emotional aspects. Cognitive empathy is about understanding another person's thoughts and feelings, while emotional empathy involves feeling what they feel. Imagine your partner had a rough day at work. Cognitive empathy helps you understand why they're stressed, while emotional empathy allows you to share in their frustration or sadness, making you a supportive companion in their emotional landscape.

Practicing empathic listening is a powerful way to cultivate both forms of empathy in your relationship. Unlike ordinary listening, empathic listening focuses on truly understanding your partner's feelings without rushing to offer solutions or judgments. Start by giving your full attention to your partner when they speak, maintaining eye contact, and nodding to show you're engaged. When they express their feelings, resist the urge to jump in with advice or opinions. Instead, reflect their emotions back to them. For instance, if they say, "I'm so frustrated with my job," you might respond with, "It sounds like you're really feeling stuck right now." This simple act of validation can make your partner feel heard and understood, deepening your emotional connection.

Empathy plays a transformative role in conflict resolution within a relationship. Consider a situation where you and your partner are arguing about household chores. Without empathy, the conversation might quickly escalate into a blame game. However, by actively seeking to understand your partner's perspective—perhaps they feel overwhelmed by other responsibilities, and chores are adding to their stress—you can shift the focus from confrontation to collaboration. Recognizing and acknowledging their feelings can lead to quicker, more effective resolutions. For example, you might say, "I can see that you're feeling really overwhelmed right now. How can we adjust our chores to make things easier for both of us?" This approach not only resolves the conflict but also strengthens your bond through mutual understanding.

However, practicing empathy isn't always straightforward. Various barriers can make it challenging, such as stress, past traumas, or differing communication styles. When you're stressed, it's easy to become self-focused and less attuned to your partner's needs. Past traumas can also affect your ability to empathize, as unresolved emotional baggage might cloud your perception. Differing communication styles can create misunderstandings, making it harder to grasp each other's feelings accurately. To overcome these challenges:

1. Start by managing your stress through techniques like mindfulness or exercise, which can help you stay present and open.
2. Address past traumas by seeking professional help if needed, as healing these wounds can improve your capacity for empathy.
3. Strive to understand and adapt to your partner's communication style, which might involve asking clarifying questions or using more explicit expressions of your own feelings.

Embracing empathy in your relationship is like opening a window to your partner's inner world. It allows you to share in their joys, sorrows, and everything in between, creating a rich tapestry of shared emotional experiences. This mutual understanding enhances your connection and builds a resilient foundation that can weather the inevitable storms of life together.

2.3 Daily Habits to Enhance Emotional Connection

In the hustle and bustle of daily life, it's easy for couples to become so engrossed in their routines that they forget to check in with each other emotionally. Establishing daily or weekly emotional check-ins can be a powerful way to ensure that lines of communication remain open, preventing the build-up of unspoken issues. These check-ins don't need to be lengthy or formal; a simple "How are you feeling today?" can go a long way. The key is to make these moments a regular part of your routine, ideally at a time when both of you are relaxed and free from distractions. This habit of touching base can help you stay connected and address minor concerns before they grow into larger problems, fostering a sense of mutual support and understanding.

Expressing appreciation and gratitude on a regular basis is another effective way to enhance emotional connection. It's easy to take each other for granted, especially when you're juggling work, family, and other responsibilities. Yet, small acts of appreciation can significantly boost relationship satisfaction and emotional closeness. This could be as simple as thanking your partner for doing the dishes or acknowledging their support during a tough day. These expressions of gratitude don't have to be grand gestures; even a heartfelt "I appreciate you" can make a big difference. When you make it a habit to recognize and verbalize what you value in your partner, it reinforces positive behaviors and deepens your emotional bond.

Engaging in shared activities that both partners enjoy can also strengthen your relationship and create lasting, positive memories. Activities can range from cooking a meal together, going for a hike, or even just watching a favorite TV show (and leave your phones in the other room!). The important thing is to connect, laugh, and enjoy each other's company. The aim is to find activities that you both enjoy and make time for them regularly, as these shared experiences can fortify your emotional connection.

Mindfulness practices like joint meditation or yoga can also play a significant role in enhancing your emotional connection. These practices help you stay present and reduce stress, making it easier to connect with your partner on a deeper level. Joint meditation sessions can be as simple as sitting quietly together and focusing on your breath for a few minutes each day. Eye gazing, another beneficial practice, involves sitting facing each other and softly gazing into each other's eyes without speaking. This can be done for a few minutes and helps build trust, intimacy, and a deep non-verbal connection. Yoga can be a fantastic way to not only stay fit but also to synchronize your movements and breathing, fostering a sense of unity and calm. These activities encourage you to be fully present with each other, allowing for a break from the constant distractions of daily life. Over time, incorporating mindfulness practices into your routine can help you both develop a more profound sense of peace and connection.

By weaving these daily habits into your relationship, you create ongoing opportunities to connect emotionally. This consistent effort to check in, express appreciation, share enjoyable activities, and practice mindfulness can transform your relationship, making it more resilient and deeply fulfilling. Emotional connection isn't built overnight; it's the result of small, intentional actions taken every day. Through these practices, you can cultivate a relationship that withstands the test of time and thrives in the face of life's inevitable challenges.

2.4 Using Love Languages to Connect Deeply

Have you ever felt like you and your partner were speaking different languages when it comes to showing love? This feeling is quite common and can be explained through the concept of love languages. Developed by Dr Gary Chapman, the idea of love languages suggests that people have different ways of expressing and receiving love. There are five primary love languages:

- Quality time
- Words of affirmation
- Acts of service
- Physical touch
- Receiving gifts

Each person has a preferred love language that makes them feel most loved and appreciated. To identify your and your partner's love languages, you can start with a simple quiz or reflection exercise. Ask yourselves what actions or words from your partner make you feel most loved. Is it when they spend uninterrupted time with you, when they compliment you, or perhaps when they help with chores without being asked?

Once you've identified your love languages, applying them in daily life can significantly enhance your emotional connection. For those whose love language is quality time, setting aside dedicated moments to be fully present with your partner can be incredibly meaningful. This might involve planning regular date nights, engaging in shared hobbies, or simply having a deep conversation without distractions. If words of affirmation are your partner's love language, make a conscious effort to offer genuine compliments and verbal expressions of love regularly. Saying "I love you," "I appreciate you," or acknowledging their efforts can go a long way in making them feel valued.

For those who resonate with acts of service, showing love through helpful actions can be powerful. This could be as simple as making their favorite breakfast, taking over a household chore they dislike, or running an errand for them. These acts demonstrate your commitment and care through tangible efforts. If physical touch is your partner's primary love language, physical affection like holding hands, hugging, or a gentle touch on the shoulder can convey deep love and connection. Finally, if receiving gifts is their love language, thoughtful gifts, whether big or small, can make them feel appreciated. It's not about the monetary value but the thought and effort behind the gesture.

Understanding and applying love languages often requires shifts in personal habits and expectations. It's about learning to express love in ways that may not come naturally to you but are deeply meaningful to your partner. This process involves ongoing communication and flexibility. For example, if your love language is physical touch but your partner's is acts of service, you'll need to consciously make an effort to perform acts of service, even if it's not your instinctual way of showing love. Discussing these adjustments openly can help both partners understand and support each other's needs better.

As you incorporate love languages into your relationship, it's important to regularly evaluate their impact. Observe how your partner responds and discuss any changes in your emotional connection. Are there improvements in how you both feel understood and appreciated? Have conflicts decreased or become easier to navigate? This iterative approach allows you to refine how you express love, ensuring it remains effective and meaningful. Regular check-ins about love languages can also be a great way to keep the conversation about emotional needs ongoing, preventing misunderstandings and fostering a deeper connection.

Through the practice of identifying, applying, and evaluating love languages, you can create a more empathetic and responsive relationship environment. This chapter has equipped you with tools to enhance your emotional connection by understanding and meeting each other's unique needs. As we progress, we'll explore more strategies to build a resilient and fulfilling partnership.

THREE

Conflict Resolution Strategies

Have you ever found yourself in the middle of a disagreement, feeling completely bewildered about how you got there in the first place? Conflicts can often seem to erupt out of nowhere, leaving both partners feeling frustrated and confused. The reality is that most conflicts have underlying triggers that, when recognized and understood, can be managed more effectively. These triggers can range from financial stress, jealousy, and differing values to seemingly minor issues that have been allowed to fester over time. Identifying these triggers is the first step in addressing them proactively and preventing them from escalating into larger conflicts.

In addition to identifying external triggers, it's also important to recognize how we respond to feedback during conflicts. Often, when we hear difficult feedback, our reactions are triggered in one of three ways:

1. **TRUTH TRIGGER:** We react to the content of the feedback, especially if it challenges what we believe to be true.
2. **RELATIONSHIP TRIGGER:** We become defensive based on who is giving the feedback, particularly if there's underlying tension with that person.
3. **IDENTITY TRIGGER:** The feedback feels like an attack on how we see ourselves, affecting our self-worth or identity.

By understanding these types of feedback triggers, couples can approach disagreements with more self-awareness and compassion. This awareness allows both partners to manage their reactions and focus on resolving the issue at hand, rather than getting stuck in defensiveness or frustration.

3.1 Identifying the Root Causes of Conflicts

Financial stress is a common trigger in many relationships. Money issues can create an atmosphere of tension and anxiety, making it easier for small disagreements to spiral into full-blown arguments. It's important to have open and honest conversations about finances, setting clear goals and boundaries. Jealousy, whether it stems from past relationships or current insecurities, can also be a significant source of conflict. Addressing jealousy involves building trust and openly discussing feelings of insecurity without the worry of judgment from your partner. Differing values, such as how you each view family obligations, career ambitions, or even political beliefs, can create friction if not properly managed. Recognizing these differences and finding common ground or respectful compromises is crucial for maintaining harmony.

Reflective listening is a powerful tool that can help uncover the deeper issues underlying surface complaints or criticisms. This technique involves truly listening to your partner's words and then reflecting their feelings back to them. For example, if your partner says, "You never help around the house," instead of becoming defensive, you might respond with, "It sounds like you're feeling overwhelmed with the household chores and need more support." This approach validates their feelings and opens the door for more meaningful conversations about underlying concerns.

Damaging communication patterns can significantly harm a relationship, often without either partner realizing it. Frequent misunderstandings, where one or both partners feel perpetually unheard or misinterpreted, can lead to frustration and resentment. Escalating disagreements, where minor issues quickly blow up into major conflicts, are another red flag. Emotional withdrawal, where one partner shuts down emotionally and disengages from the conversation, can create a sense of isolation and neglect. Lastly, a pervasive feeling of not being heard or valued can erode the foundation of any relationship. Identifying these patterns early is crucial to prevent further harm.

To better understand and address these patterns, self-assessment tools can be incredibly helpful. One effective method is to take a communication survey together, asking questions about how often you feel misunderstood, the frequency and intensity of your disagreements, and whether you feel heard and valued by your partner. Analyzing the results can provide insights into specific areas that need improvement. For instance, if you both frequently feel misunderstood, it might indicate a need to work on clearer and more empathetic communication.

Mapping out recurring conflict patterns can also shed light on the root causes of your disagreements. Start by keeping a conflict journal where you record each argument, noting the trigger, how it escalated, and how it was resolved. Over time, you may notice patterns that point to deeper issues. For example, you might realize that most of your arguments occur when discussing financial matters, indicating that financial stress is a significant trigger. Understanding these patterns can help you address the underlying issues more effectively.

Individual backgrounds play a significant role in how each partner approaches conflicts. Family dynamics, past relationships, and personal values all influence your behavior and reactions. For instance, if you grew up in a household where conflicts were resolved through yelling, you might find yourself defaulting to that behavior. Conversely, if your partner was raised in an environment where conflicts were avoided at all costs, they might be more likely to withdraw. Acknowledging these influences can help you understand each other's perspectives and develop more effective conflict-resolution strategies.

Reflective Exercise: Conflict Mapping

Take some time to map out your recent conflicts. Note down each disagreement, identifying the trigger, how it escalated, and the resolution. Look for patterns—are there common themes or recurring issues? Discuss your findings with your partner and explore how understanding these patterns can address the root causes of your conflicts more effectively. This exercise can provide valuable insights and pave the way for healthier communication and conflict resolution in your relationship.

3.2 Techniques for Healthy Argumentation

Arguments are an inevitable part of any relationship, but how you handle them can make all the difference. Setting ground rules before an argument begins can create a safer, more constructive environment. Imagine starting a discussion by agreeing that no name-calling will be tolerated. This simple rule helps keep the conversation respectful and focused on the issue at hand rather than descending into personal attacks. Another crucial ground rule is taking turns speaking. Interruptions can escalate tensions, so allowing each person to fully express their thoughts before the other responds can lead to more productive discussions. Keeping the conversation focused on one issue at a time is also vital. It's easy to get sidetracked and bring up past grievances, but this only muddles the current issue and can make the argument feel overwhelming. However, it is important to take note of the past grievances, as this indicates an unresolved problem. Therefore, it is helpful to work through these grievances in a different context. But by sticking to one topic, you can work towards a resolution more effectively.

Constructive arguments are about finding solutions rather than dwelling on problems. For example, if you're upset that your partner didn't help with dinner, a destructive approach might be to accuse them of being lazy or uncaring. This only puts them on the defensive. Instead, a constructive approach would be to express how their lack of help made you feel and propose a solution. You might say, "I felt really overwhelmed making dinner alone tonight. Can we come up with a plan for sharing this responsibility?" This shifts the focus from blame to collaboration, making it easier for your partner to respond positively and work towards a solution with you.

Using "I" statements instead of "you" statements is another powerful technique for reducing defensiveness in arguments. When you say, "You never listen to me," it immediately puts your partner on the defensive and makes them feel attacked. Instead, try saying, "I feel unheard when I don't get a chance to share my thoughts." This subtle shift in language focuses on your feelings rather than accusing your partner, making it easier for them to understand your perspective without feeling blamed. Over time, this practice can transform the way you communicate during conflicts, making it easier to resolve issues without escalating tensions.

Negotiation and compromise are the backbones of any healthy relationship. It's crucial to recognize that both partners have needs and perspectives that deserve respect. Start by clearly stating your own needs and listening to your partner's needs in return. For example, if you want to spend more time together but your partner values their alone time, acknowledge both needs without dismissing either. You might say, "I understand that you need time alone to recharge, and I also need quality time with you to feel connected. Can we find a balance that works for both of us?" This approach opens the door to finding a compromise that respects both partners' needs.

Finding a middle ground often requires creativity and flexibility. Maybe it means scheduling specific nights for quality time and others for personal space. The key is to approach negotiation with the mindset that you are on the same team, working together to find a solution that benefits both of you. This collaborative approach can turn potential conflicts into opportunities for deeper understanding and stronger connection.

Interactive Exercise: Negotiation Practice

Take a moment to practice negotiation with your partner on a low-stakes issue. Choose a minor disagreement, like what to watch on TV or where to go for dinner. Each partner should state their preference and the underlying reason for it. Then, discuss possible compromises that address both preferences. This exercise builds your negotiation skills in a low-pressure environment, making it easier to handle more significant issues when they arise.

Healthy argumentation is not about avoiding conflicts but managing them in ways that lead to growth and understanding. By setting ground rules, using constructive techniques, and practicing negotiation and compromise, you can navigate disagreements in a way that strengthens, rather than weakens, your relationship.

3.3 Preventing Escalation: Timeout Techniques

In the heat of an argument, recognizing the signs of escalation can be a game-changer. Physical indicators like raised voices, rapid breathing, or clenched fists are often the first clues that a discussion is starting to spiral out of control. Emotionally, you might notice a surge of anger, frustration, or even defensiveness. These signs are your body's way of signaling that it's time to pause and reassess before things get worse. When you catch these signals early, you can take proactive steps to prevent the argument from escalating further. This awareness not only helps in managing your own reactions but also in understanding your partner's emotional state, creating a more empathetic environment.

Implementing timeout protocols can be a lifesaver in such moments. The idea is to mutually agree on taking a break when either partner feels that the argument is getting too heated. This isn't about avoiding the issue but rather about taking a necessary pause to cool down and gather your thoughts. When you both agree to a timeout, it's important to set a specific duration for the break, whether it's 15 minutes or an hour. During this time, avoid ruminating on the argument or planning your next point. Instead, focus on calming down and gaining perspective. This break allows both partners to return to the conversation with a clearer, calmer mindset, making it easier to address the issue constructively.

During the timeout, calming strategies can be incredibly effective. Deep breathing exercises, where you inhale deeply for a count of four, hold for four, and exhale for four, can slow your heart rate and reduce anxiety. Meditation is another powerful tool that can center your mind and bring a sense of peace. Even a brief five-minute meditation can reset your emotional state. Physical activities like going for a walk or doing light stretching can also work wonders. These activities help release pent-up energy and tension, making it easier to return to the discussion with a more balanced and open attitude. The key is to find what works best for you and make it a part of your timeout routine.

Resuming discussions, post-timeout, requires a thoughtful approach to ensure that both partners feel calm and ready to engage productively. Start by acknowledging the timeout and expressing appreciation for each other's willingness to take a break. This sets a positive tone for the conversation. Then, gently reintroduce the topic, focusing on one issue at a time. It's crucial to maintain a calm and respectful tone, even if the subject matter is sensitive. If you notice the conversation starting to escalate again, don't hesitate to suggest another short break. The goal is to keep the discussion constructive and solution-oriented rather than letting it devolve into another argument.

By incorporating these timeout techniques into your conflict resolution toolkit, you can create a more supportive and understanding dynamic in your relationship. This approach helps in managing immediate conflicts and also builds a foundation for healthier communication habits in the long run. Recognizing the signs of escalation, agreeing on timeout protocols, employing calming strategies, and thoughtfully resuming discussions can transform the way you navigate disagreements, fostering a deeper sense of connection and mutual respect.

3.4 After the Argument: Steps to Reconciliation

After the dust of an argument has settled, the immediate steps you take can significantly influence the path to reconciliation. It's crucial to start by mutually acknowledging the conflict and any hurt feelings that may have arisen. This goal is to validate each other's experiences. A simple "I realize we both got hurt during that argument" can go a long way. This mutual acknowledgment sets a foundation of empathy and understanding, which is essential for moving forward constructively.

Once the initial emotions have calmed, discussing the lessons learned from the argument can be incredibly insightful. This is an opportunity to reflect on what the conflict revealed about each other's perspectives and needs. For instance, you might realize that the argument highlighted a recurring issue, such as feeling unappreciated or misunderstood. Discussing these insights helps both partners gain a deeper understanding of each other, which can prevent similar conflicts in the future. The goal is to identify what went wrong and recognize what can be improved. This reflective conversation should be approached with a sense of curiosity and openness rather than blame or defensiveness.

Restorative actions are the next step in mending any emotional distance that may have developed during the argument. These actions can take many forms, depending on what feels meaningful to you and your partner. Specific apologies are a powerful way to show genuine remorse and a willingness to make amends. Instead of a generic "I'm sorry," try saying, "I'm sorry for raising my voice and not listening to what you were trying to say." Acts of kindness can also help rebuild the emotional bridge. This could be as simple as making a favorite meal, offering a heartfelt compliment, or spending quality time together. These gestures not only show that you care and are committed to nurturing the relationship but also align with different love languages, whether it's acts of service, words of affirmation, or quality time. By recognizing and speaking your partner's love language through these small acts, you can reinforce the bond and demonstrate your understanding of what makes them feel loved and valued.

Building a resilience plan is an essential step to ensure that future conflicts are handled more effectively. Reflect on the techniques and strategies that worked well during the resolution process and consider how they can be applied to future disagreements. For example, if taking a timeout helped de-escalate the argument, make it a part of your conflict resolution toolkit. Discuss and agree on a set of strategies that you both feel comfortable with, such as setting ground rules for arguments, using "I" statements, and practicing active listening. This plan serves as a roadmap for navigating conflicts, making it easier to maintain a healthy and respectful dynamic.

To reinforce these strategies, consider creating a visual reminder, such as a conflict resolution checklist or a set of agreed-upon rules, that you can refer to during heated moments. This tangible reference can help keep both partners on track and committed to the agreed-upon methods. The goal is to build a partnership where conflicts are seen as opportunities for growth and understanding rather than threats to the relationship's stability. This proactive approach strengthens your bond and equips you with the tools to handle life's inevitable challenges together.

By taking immediate steps post-argument, discussing lessons learned, engaging in restorative actions, and building a resilience plan, you create a robust framework for navigating conflicts. This chapter has provided you with the strategies and insights needed to turn arguments into opportunities for deeper connection and mutual growth. As we move forward, we'll delve into more nuanced aspects of relationship dynamics, providing you with additional tools to foster a healthy and fulfilling partnership.

FOUR

Trust Building and Maintenance

H ave you ever wondered why trust seems so fragile yet so fundamental in relationships? Trust forms the bedrock of any meaningful connection, and without it, even the most passionate love can falter. In a romantic relationship, trust transcends the mere belief that your partner won't betray you; it encompasses emotional safety, mutual reliability, and the assurance that both partners have each other's best interests at heart. But what exactly does trust mean in this context?

4.1 The Fundamentals of Trust

Trust in a romantic relationship can be seen as a multifaceted concept involving both emotional and practical dimensions. Emotionally, trust means feeling secure enough to open up about your innermost thoughts and vulnerabilities, and the ability to be your "true self", knowing that your partner will respond with empathy rather than judgment. It's the belief that your partner will support you through life's ups and downs, valuing your feelings and experiences as much as their own. Practically, trust involves dependability and integrity—knowing that your partner will follow through on their promises and be consistent in their actions. Imagine a scenario where you rely on your partner to pick you up from work. Trust is knowing they'll be there on time, but it's also about feeling understood and supported if they need to reschedule due to unforeseen circumstances.

Building trust is akin to constructing a sturdy house; it requires a solid foundation and reliable materials. Consistency is one of the essential elements in this construction. Consistency in actions and words helps establish a predictable and stable environment where both partners know what to expect from each other. For instance, if you always discuss your day during dinner, breaking that routine without explanation could create uncertainty. Reliability goes hand in hand with consistency. When you say you'll do something, following through reinforces your trustworthiness. If you promise to handle the grocery shopping, doing it consistently builds your partner's confidence in relying on you. Integrity, the third pillar, involves being honest and transparent, even when it's uncomfortable. It means owning up to your mistakes and being truthful about your intentions. An example might be admitting that you spent more money than planned and discussing how to manage it together rather than hiding the overspend.

Assessing the current level of trust in your relationship is a crucial step in identifying areas for improvement. Start by reflecting on specific aspects of your relationship where trust might be tested. Do you feel secure sharing your deepest fears with your partner? Can you rely on them to be there when they say they will? If you find certain areas lacking, it's essential to address these vulnerabilities openly. One practical way to assess trust is through a trust audit. Create a list of scenarios and rate your confidence in your partner's reliability and emotional support in each one. For example, you might rate your trust in their financial responsibility or their ability to keep your confidence. This exercise can highlight strengths and areas needing attention, providing a roadmap for building stronger trust.

Laying a strong foundation of trust early in a relationship sets the stage for long-term stability. Small, consistent actions often carry more weight than grand gestures or verbal promises. Simple acts like regularly checking in with each other, showing up on time, and sharing your thoughts and feelings build a reservoir of trust over time. It's like adding bricks to a wall, each one reinforcing the structure. When you consistently demonstrate that you're reliable and emotionally available, it becomes easier for your partner to trust you. For instance, if you make it a habit to discuss your plans and decisions with your partner, it shows that you value their input and are committed to transparency.

Building trust requires ongoing effort and intentionality. It's about creating a pattern of behavior that your partner can depend on, fostering an environment of mutual respect and understanding. This foundation will not only help you navigate inevitable challenges but also strengthen the emotional bond that holds your relationship together. Trust is a continuous process of showing up, being honest, and supporting each other through life's many twists and turns.

⊏⊐

Trust Audit Exercise

Take a moment to conduct a trust audit with your partner. List out various scenarios such as financial decisions, emotional support, keeping promises, and handling conflicts. Rate your confidence in each area on a scale from 1 to 10. Discuss the ratings together, identifying areas of strength and those needing improvement. This exercise will give you a clearer picture of your trust landscape and help you focus on building a stronger, more reliable foundation.

To guide you through this process, you can use the following Trust Audit Worksheet. This tool offers a structured approach to rating key areas of trust in your relationship, making it easier to assess your strengths and identify areas for improvement. Use it as a starting point for meaningful conversations with your partner and work together to build a stronger foundation of trust.

⊏⊐

Trust Audit Worksheet

The purpose of this worksheet helps you and your partner assess the current level of trust in your relationship by identifying strengths and areas that need improvement. By reflecting on key aspects of your partnership, you can create a roadmap for building stronger trust.

1. Together with your partner (or on your own if preferred), go through each scenario listed below.
2. Rate your confidence in your partner's reliability and emotional support on a scale from 1 to 10, with 1 being "I don't trust them in this area at all" and 10 being "I completely trust them."

3. After completing the audit, discuss your scores with your partner, focusing on areas where trust might need reinforcement and recognizing your strengths.

EMOTIONAL VULNERABILITY:

I feel comfortable sharing my deepest fears, insecurities, and desires with my partner.
Rating: ___ / 10

RELIABILITY:

I trust that my partner will follow through when they make commitments, such as being on time or fulfilling promises.
Rating: ___ / 10

FINANCIAL RESPONSIBILITY:

I trust my partner to manage financial matters responsibly and transparently.
Rating: ___ / 10

COMMUNICATION:

I trust my partner to be honest and open with me, even when discussing difficult or uncomfortable topics.
Rating: ___ / 10

CONFLICT RESOLUTION:

I trust my partner to handle disagreements respectfully and with the intention of finding a solution.
Rating: ___ / 10

LOYALTY:

I trust that my partner remains faithful and committed to me.
Rating: ___ / 10

Emotional Support:

I trust my partner to be there for me emotionally when I need support or comfort.

Rating: ___ / 10

Reflection Questions:

- Which areas did you score the highest in? Celebrate those strengths!
- Where did you score lower? Why do you think trust is more fragile in these areas?
- What steps can you and your partner take to strengthen trust in these areas?

4.2 Rebuilding Trust After Betrayal

Betrayal. Just the word itself can bring a rush of emotions and even a physical response. When someone you love breaks your trust, the impact can be both profound and far-reaching. Betrayal can manifest in various forms, from infidelity and lies to financial deceit or emotional manipulation. Regardless of how it occurs, the emotional fallout is often similar: a whirlwind of hurt, anger, confusion, and disillusionment. You might find yourself questioning everything you thought you knew about your partner and your relationship. This breach of trust can lead to a profound sense of loss, as the safety and security you once felt are shattered. Rebuilding trust after such a deep wound is challenging, but it's not impossible.

The first step in rebuilding trust after betrayal is to openly acknowledge what happened. This involves a candid conversation where the betraying partner takes full responsibility for their actions without making excuses or shifting blame. An honest and heartfelt apology is crucial here, one that acknowledges the pain caused and expresses genuine remorse. It's not enough to simply say, "I'm sorry"; the apology must reflect a deep understanding of the impact of the betrayal. Following this, there must be a commitment to repair the relationship. This means both partners agree to invest the time and effort needed to heal and rebuild trust. Actions speak louder than words, so consistent behavior that aligns with this commitment is vital.

Forgiveness plays a pivotal role in the trust restoration process. Forgiveness is not about condoning the betrayal or forgetting that it happened. Instead, it's about letting go of the intense anger and resentment that can hinder healing. Forgiveness can be given when the betrayed partner feels ready, and it should never be rushed. It's a personal journey that may take time, and that's okay. The benefits of forgiveness are numerous; it can lighten the emotional burden, reduce stress, and open the door to genuine reconciliation. However, it's important to recognize its limits. Forgiveness does not erase the need for accountability or the necessity for the betraying partner to demonstrate consistent, trustworthy behavior moving forward.

Monitoring the healing process is essential for both partners. Regular check-ins can track progress and address any lingering concerns or setbacks. These check-ins should be open and honest, allowing both partners to express their feelings and needs as they navigate this complex terrain. Adjustments to the rebuilding strategies may be necessary as new challenges or revelations come to light. It's important to remain flexible and patient, understanding that healing is not linear and setbacks may occur. These moments should be seen as opportunities for further growth and understanding rather than failures.

To aid in this process, consider establishing a set of guidelines or agreements that outline how you will both work towards rebuilding trust. This might include specific actions the betraying partner will take to demonstrate their commitment, such as attending therapy, being more transparent, or actively working on communication skills. For the betrayed partner, it might involve setting boundaries and expressing needs clearly. Both partners should agree on these guidelines together, ensuring they are realistic and supportive of the healing process. Regularly revisiting these agreements can help keep both partners accountable and focused on their shared goal of rebuilding trust.

Rebuilding trust after betrayal is undoubtedly one of the most challenging tasks a couple can face. It requires a deep commitment to healing, open communication, and a willingness to forgive. By acknowledging the impact of the betrayal, taking concrete steps to repair the relationship, embracing forgiveness, and closely monitoring progress, couples can navigate this difficult path. Trust can be rebuilt, and relationships can emerge stronger and more resilient than before.

4.3 Transparency and Honesty Exercises

Creating an environment where honesty thrives requires deliberate effort and consistent practice. To foster such an environment, it's crucial to establish a safe space where both partners feel encouraged to share their thoughts and feelings without fear of judgment or retaliation. This starts with setting clear expectations about the importance of honesty in your relationship. Discuss openly what honesty means to each of you and agree on the principles you both will uphold. Consider implementing practical exercises like weekly check-ins, where you both take turns sharing something that has been on your mind. These check-ins should be framed as opportunities for connection rather than confrontation, ensuring that both partners feel respected, heard, and valued.

Role-playing scenarios can be an effective way to practice honesty in a controlled setting, preparing you for real-life situations. Create hypothetical scenarios that test your ability to be transparent with each other. For instance, one partner might role-play a situation where they need to disclose a mistake they made at work that affects the family, while the other practices responding with empathy and support. Switch roles and try different scenarios, such as discussing financial worries or expressing feelings of neglect. This exercise not only builds your confidence in handling difficult conversations but also helps you understand each other's communication styles and emotional triggers, making it easier to navigate similar situations in real life.

Incorporating daily or weekly honesty practices into your routine can create a habit of transparency. One such practice is the 'truth moment,' a designated time when both partners share something they feel vulnerable about. This could be anything from admitting to feeling overwhelmed by work to expressing fears about the future. The key is to listen without interrupting or judging, allowing each other to fully express and process these feelings. Over time, these truth moments can build a deeper sense of trust and intimacy as you both become more comfortable sharing your innermost thoughts and emotions. Another practice could be leaving each other small notes or messages that express appreciation or address minor concerns in a gentle way, fostering ongoing open communication.

Building a culture of honesty in your relationship involves more than just individual practices; it requires a collective commitment to transparency and mutual respect. Set clear expectations about honesty and lead by example. If you expect your partner to be open and truthful, you must also be willing to be vulnerable and transparent. This means admitting when you're wrong, acknowledging your mistakes, and being open about your feelings and intentions. Consistently demonstrating these behaviors can encourage your partner to do the same. Additionally, celebrate moments of honesty and openness, recognizing the courage it takes to be vulnerable. Positive reinforcement can strengthen these behaviors, making honesty a natural and integral part of your relationship.

To further reinforce a culture of honesty, consider creating a set of shared values or a relationship mission statement that highlights the importance of transparency. Discuss and write down these values together, placing them somewhere visible as a constant reminder of your commitment. Regularly revisit and revise these values as your relationship evolves, ensuring they remain relevant and meaningful. Engaging in activities that promote mutual understanding, such as couples therapy or workshops, can also provide valuable tools and insights for maintaining honesty. By intentionally cultivating an environment where honesty is encouraged and rewarded, you lay the groundwork for a relationship built on trust, respect, and deep emotional connection.

4.4 Maintaining Trust Through Life's Challenges

Life has a way of throwing curveballs, and these unexpected events can test the strength of your relationship's trust. Financial hardships, for instance, can place a significant strain on a couple. The stress of financial instability can lead to arguments about spending habits, debt, and financial priorities. During these times, it's crucial to maintain open lines of communication and work collaboratively to find solutions. Health changes, whether chronic illness or sudden medical emergencies, can also test trust. When one partner becomes a caregiver, the dynamic shifts, requiring patience, empathy, and a recalibration of roles. Long periods apart due to work commitments or travel can introduce feelings of isolation and insecurity, making it vital to reinforce trust through regular, meaningful communication.

Adapting trust-building practices to fit changing circumstances is key to ensuring that trust grows, rather than erodes, during tough times. One effective strategy is to establish new routines that accommodate the current situation. If financial hardship is the issue, creating a transparent budgeting plan together can foster a sense of teamwork and mutual responsibility. For health-related challenges, setting up a caregiving schedule that includes self-care for the caregiver can prevent burnout and resentment. When facing long periods apart, technology can be a lifeline— using video calls, instant messaging, and shared online calendars can help maintain a sense of connection and involvement in each other's lives. Adaptability is about finding new ways to uphold the principles of trust— reliability, consistency, and integrity—despite the changing landscape.

Having a support system outside the relationship is equally important. Friends, family, or support groups can provide a sounding board, offer advice, or simply be there to listen. This external support can alleviate some of the pressure on the relationship, allowing each partner to recharge emotionally. For instance, talking to a trusted friend about your financial worries can provide new perspectives and solutions, reducing the tension between you and your partner. However, it's essential that both partners feel comfortable with sensitive relationship information being shared with an outside party. Some people are open to this, while others may feel more hesitant, so it's important to discuss and respect each other's boundaries. In health crises, family members can step in to help with caregiving duties, giving the primary caregiver some much-needed respite. Utilizing these external networks can strengthen the internal bond, as both partners feel supported and less isolated in their struggles.

Continuously assessing and rebuilding trust is a proactive approach that can prevent small issues from becoming insurmountable problems. Regularly check in with each other about the state of your trust, discussing any concerns or areas where you feel improvement is needed. This might involve setting aside monthly or quarterly "trust talks," where you both reflect on recent events and how they have impacted your sense of trust. Use these discussions to celebrate successes and address any lapses. For instance, if one partner feels that trust has been compromised due to missed commitments, discuss why it happened and how to prevent it in the future. This ongoing dialogue keeps trust at the forefront of your relationship, making it easier to address issues before they escalate.

Rebuilding trust continuously also involves being willing to make adjustments as needed. Life is dynamic, and what worked at one stage of your relationship might not be effective later on. Be open to revisiting and revising your trust-building strategies, whether it's updating your communication methods, redefining roles within the relationship, or seeking professional guidance through therapy. This flexibility ensures that your approach to trust remains relevant and effective, adapting to the evolving needs and circumstances of both partners.

Maintaining trust through life's challenges is about being proactive, adaptable, and supported. By anticipating common challenges, adapting trust-building practices, leveraging external support systems, and continuously assessing and rebuilding trust, you can navigate even the toughest times together. The next chapter will delve into the dynamics of maintaining intimacy and connection, further strengthening the foundation of your relationship.

FIVE

Strengthening Intimacy and Connection

Have you ever wondered why some simple gestures can make you feel closer to your partner while, at other times, they seem to fall flat? The power of physical touch in relationships is often underestimated, yet it is one of the most vital components of emotional intimacy. Studies have shown that physical touch can reduce stress, lower blood pressure, and even strengthen the immune system. But beyond the physiological benefits, touch communicates love, comfort, and security in ways that words alone often cannot.

5.1 The Importance of Physical Touch

Touch plays a crucial role in relationships, serving as a silent yet powerful communicator of emotions. When partners engage in physical touch, it releases oxytocin, often referred to as the "love hormone," which promotes feelings of bonding and trust. Imagine the comfort of a hug after a long day or the simple act of holding hands while walking through a park. These small gestures can create a profound sense of connection and reassurance. Touch isn't just about physical pleasure; it conveys support, empathy, and affection. For instance, a gentle touch on the arm during a difficult conversation can communicate understanding and solidarity, making the exchange more emotionally resonant.

Non-sexual touches, such as hand-holding, hugging, and cuddling, are essential for maintaining a physical connection in daily life. These forms of touch are often overlooked but play a significant role in reinforcing the emotional bond between partners. Hand-holding, for example, can serve as a reassuring gesture that signifies unity and presence. Hugging, on the other hand, can provide a full-body embrace that offers a sense of security and warmth. Cuddling, whether it's on the couch while watching a movie or in bed before falling asleep, allows for prolonged physical closeness, which can enhance feelings of love and attachment. These simple yet meaningful touches should be woven into the fabric of your daily interactions to keep the connection strong and vibrant.

However, not everyone finds physical touch easy or comfortable. Past trauma, personal boundaries, or differing touch preferences can create barriers to physical intimacy. If you or your partner struggle with physical touch, it's important to approach the topic with sensitivity and understanding. Start by having an open conversation about your touch preferences and any discomfort you may feel. Gradually increasing comfort levels with physical contact can make a significant difference. Begin with small, non-threatening touches like a pat on the back or a brief hand squeeze. Over time, as trust and comfort grow, you can introduce more prolonged forms of touch, always respecting each other's boundaries and comfort zones. This gradual approach builds a safe and consensual environment for physical intimacy.

Touch can also serve as a powerful form of non-verbal communication, enhancing your ability to express emotions and read each other's emotional states. For instance, a soft caress can convey tenderness and love, while a firm grip can communicate strength and support. By paying attention to your partner's physical cues, you can gain insights into their emotional state, even when they find it difficult to articulate their feelings. This skill of reading and responding to non-verbal cues can deepen your emotional connection and improve overall communication. It's about tuning into the subtle language of touch and using it to create a more empathetic and responsive relationship dynamic.

⊏⊐

Interactive Exercise: Touch Map

Create a "touch map" with your partner. Take a large sheet of paper and draw simple outlines of your bodies. Mark areas where you enjoy being touched, areas you are neutral about, and areas that are off-limits. Use different colors to indicate each category. Discuss the map together, explaining your preferences and listening to your partner's. This exercise can help you understand and respect each other's boundaries while finding new ways to connect physically.

5.2 Emotional Intimacy Through Shared Experiences

Creating shared goals and dreams can be a powerful way to bring couples closer together, fostering a sense of teamwork and mutual aspiration. Imagine the joy of planning a trip together, from choosing the destination to mapping out the itinerary. This process involves collaboration, compromise, and excitement, all of which can strengthen your bond. Whether it's a weekend getaway or a month-long adventure, the anticipation and planning can be just as enriching as the trip itself. Similarly, starting a new hobby together, like cooking classes or gardening, can provide regular opportunities for connection and shared accomplishment. Working on a home project, such as redecorating a room or building a garden, not only enhances your living space but also gives you a tangible result of your joint efforts. These shared goals and dreams create a sense of unity and purpose, making your relationship a partnership in the truest sense.

Establishing rituals of connection is another effective way to deepen emotional intimacy. Daily or weekly rituals, no matter how small, create touchpoints that keep you connected amidst the hustle and bustle of life. Consider starting your day with a morning coffee together, a quiet moment to share your thoughts and set a positive tone for the day. Evening walks can serve as a time to unwind, talk about your day, and enjoy each other's company without distractions. Weekly date nights, whether at a fancy restaurant or a cozy night in with a movie, can keep the romance alive and give you something to look forward to together. These rituals become cherished routines that anchor your relationship, providing consistent opportunities for connection and intimacy.

Sharing vulnerabilities and fears is a profound way to deepen emotional intimacy. It's not always easy to open up about our deepest insecurities and fears, but doing so can create a powerful bond. When you share your vulnerabilities, you allow your partner to see you in a raw, unfiltered way, fostering trust, empathy, and understanding. Safe communication strategies are crucial here. Start by creating a non-judgmental space where both partners feel comfortable expressing their true feelings. Use phrases like, "I feel scared when..." or "I worry about..." to frame your vulnerabilities as personal experiences rather than accusations. Listen actively and validate each other's feelings, showing that you're there to support and understand. This mutual sharing builds a foundation of trust and emotional closeness, making your relationship more resilient and connected.

Building positive memories together is another key to strengthening emotional bonds. Engaging in activities that create joyful and meaningful experiences can serve as anchors in your relationship. Taking a class together, whether it's dancing, painting, or a cooking course, allows you to learn and grow together while having fun. Visiting new places, whether it's a local park or a distant city, provides fresh experiences and adventures that you can reminisce about for years to come. These activities enrich your relationship in the present and create a reservoir of positive memories that you can draw upon during challenging times. They serve as reminders of your shared joy and connection, reinforcing your bond.

___

Memory Building Activity: Memory Jar

Create a "Memory Jar" together. Get a large jar and decorate it to reflect your relationship. Every time you create a positive memory, write it down on a small piece of paper and place it in the jar. This could be a special date, a funny moment, or a shared accomplishment. Over time, your jar will fill with these memories, providing a visual and tangible reminder of your shared experiences. Whenever you need a boost, take a moment to read through some of the memories together, reliving the joy and connection they brought.

By focusing on shared goals, establishing meaningful rituals, embracing vulnerabilities, and building positive memories, you create a rich tapestry of emotional intimacy that strengthens your relationship in profound ways.

5.3 Rekindling Romance in Long-term Relationships

Have you ever felt like the spark in your relationship has dimmed over time? Introducing new experiences can be a game-changer that reignites that romance and breaks the monotony that often occurs in long-term relationships. Novelty brings excitement and a sense of adventure, reminding you of the thrill you felt in the early days of your relationship. This doesn't mean you have to embark on extravagant adventures; even small changes can make a big difference. Trying a new restaurant, exploring a hobby you've both been curious about, or even rearranging your living space together can inject fresh energy into your relationship. These new experiences provide opportunities to see each other in different lights and create new, shared memories, reinforcing the bond between you.

Surprises and thoughtful gestures are another powerful way to keep the romantic spark alive. The element of surprise adds a layer of excitement and anticipation, making your partner feel cherished and valued. Imagine the joy on your partner's face when they find an unexpected love note in their lunch bag or the thrill of planning a mystery date where the destination remains a secret until you arrive. These gestures don't have to be grand or expensive; it's the thought and effort that count. Perhaps you could surprise them with their favorite dessert after a long day or plan a day trip to a place they've always wanted to visit. The key is to keep it personal and thoughtful, showing that you've been paying attention to their likes and interests.

Physical attractiveness plays a significant role in sustaining attraction in long-term relationships. It's not about adhering to societal standards of beauty but about maintaining a sense of self-respect and mutual appreciation. Making an effort to stay fit, dressing well, and grooming regularly can have a positive impact on how you feel about yourself and each other. Think about how you felt when you first started dating, putting in that extra effort to look your best. Continuing to do so can reignite those initial feelings of attraction. This doesn't mean you need to be dressed to the nines all the time, but small efforts like wearing a favorite cologne or styling your hair can make a noticeable difference. Encouraging each other to stay active and healthy can also be a fun way to bond, whether it's going for a run together or joining a fitness class.

Romantic communication is the glue that holds all these elements together. It's about expressing your love and appreciation in ways that resonate with your partner. Flirtatious messages, whether it's a playful text during the day or a whispered compliment in the evening, can keep the romance alive. Compliments are powerful; they show that you notice and appreciate each other. Instead of generic phrases, be specific: "I love how you always know how to make me laugh" or "You looked stunning in that outfit today." These personalized compliments can make your partner feel truly seen and valued. Expressing affection verbally and physically reinforces these feelings, whether it's saying "I love you" frequently or giving a warm hug when you greet each other.

Interactive Exercise: Romantic Gesture Planner

Create a "Romantic Gesture Planner" together. List out small and big gestures that you both appreciate, like surprise notes, favorite meals, or weekend getaways. Use a calendar to plan these gestures throughout the year, ensuring that the romance is kept alive consistently.

Incorporating novelty, surprises, physical attractiveness, and romantic communication into your relationship can help rekindle the romance and sustain it over the long haul. These efforts show that you value and appreciate each other, creating a vibrant and loving partnership that continues to grow and flourish.

5.4 Addressing Sexual Compatibility and Challenges

Openly discussing sexual desires and preferences is crucial for maintaining a healthy and fulfilling sexual relationship. Yet, many couples find it difficult to talk about these topics without feeling embarrassment or fear of judgment. The key to fostering a healthy sexual dialogue lies in creating a safe and respectful environment where both partners feel comfortable sharing their thoughts and feelings. Start by setting aside dedicated time to talk about your sexual needs, ensuring that the conversation is free from distractions. Use "I" statements to express your desires and preferences, such as "I feel more connected to you when we try new things in the bedroom" or "I really enjoy it when you touch me this way." This approach focuses on your personal experiences rather than making your partner feel criticized. Encourage your partner to share their own desires and preferences, and listen actively to understand their perspective. The goal is to create an ongoing dialogue where both partners feel heard and valued, leading to a more satisfying and intimate sexual connection.

Mismatched libidos are a common challenge that many couples face, often leading to frustration and feelings of rejection. It's important to approach this issue with empathy and a willingness to find solutions that work for both partners. Begin by acknowledging that it's normal for sexual desire to fluctuate, and that mismatched libidos don't mean the relationship is doomed. Open communication is key. Discuss your individual needs and explore ways to compromise. For example, if one partner has a higher libido, they might suggest scheduling a regular intimate time that aligns with both partners' comfort levels. On the other hand, the partner with a lower libido can find alternate ways to connect, such as through non-sexual touch or shared activities that foster intimacy. Experimenting with different forms of intimacy can also help bridge the gap, ensuring that both partners feel satisfied and connected.

As couples age, changes in sexual function due to aging or health issues can pose new challenges. It's important to recognize that these changes are natural and can be navigated with understanding and adaptability. Openly discussing how aging affects your sexual relationship can alleviate concerns and foster a sense of partnership in finding solutions. For instance, if one partner experiences a decrease in libido due to hormonal changes, consider exploring new ways to maintain intimacy, such as focusing on extended foreplay or trying different positions that may be more comfort-able. Health issues like chronic pain or medications can also impact sexual function. In such cases, consulting a healthcare professional can provide valuable insights and potential treatments. Remember, maintaining a fulfilling sexual relationship as you age is about adapting to changes together and prioritizing emotional closeness alongside physical intimacy.

Exploring new sexual experiences within comfortable boundaries can enhance sexual compatibility and satisfaction. It's important to approach this exploration with mutual consent and respect for each other's bound-aries. Start by having an open conversation about your curiosities and interests, ensuring that both partners feel comfortable expressing their desires. Discuss what you're interested in trying and establish clear bound-aries to ensure that both partners feel safe and respected. Experimenting with new experiences can reignite passion and bring a sense of novelty to your sexual relationship. Whether it's trying a new position, introducing toys, or exploring fantasies, the key is to prioritize mutual enjoyment and consent. This exploration can deepen your connection and enhance your overall sexual satisfaction.

Communicating intimacy needs without being demanding can be a delicate balance, but it's essential for fostering a healthy and respectful relationship. Using "I" statements to express your desires can convey your needs without making your partner feel pressured or defensive. For example, saying, "I feel closer to you when we spend time together" or "I would love to share more intimate moments with you because it makes me feel connected" focuses on your feelings and experiences. Encourage honest and empathic discussions where both partners feel heard and appreciated. Reflective listening exercises can be particularly helpful in this context. Take turns sharing your intimacy needs and reflecting back what you heard to ensure understanding. This practice can deepen your relationship by creating a sense of empathy and mutual support.

In summary, addressing sexual compatibility and challenges requires open communication, empathy, and a willingness to explore new experiences together. By fostering a healthy sexual dialogue, finding compromises for mismatched libidos, adapting to changes due to aging or health issues, and respecting each other's boundaries, you can enhance your sexual relationship and strengthen your overall connection. This holistic approach ensures that both partners feel satisfied and valued, creating a fulfilling and intimate partnership.

Make a Difference with Your Review

Unlock the Power of Connection

"THE BEST WAY TO FIND YOURSELF IS TO LOSE YOURSELF IN THE SERVICE OF OTHERS." - MAHATMA GANDHI

Helping others brings joy, and your review of *From Conflict to Closeness - The Couples Therapy Playbook* can do just that. By sharing your thoughts, you can help other couples find the guidance they need to overcome emotional distance, rebuild trust, and improve communication.

So, here's a question for you...

Would you help a couple you've never met, even if you never got credit for it?

They might be struggling, just like you once were, longing for a way to make things better but not knowing where to turn.

. . .

Our mission is to make healthy relationships accessible to everyone. Everything in this book is designed to support that goal. And the only way to reach more couples is with your help.

Most people do, in fact, judge a book by its cover (and its reviews). So here's my request on behalf of a couple struggling with communication and trust:

Please help them by leaving a review for this book.

Your gift costs nothing and takes less than 60 seconds, but it could change a couple's life forever. Your review could help…
 …one more couple finds peace in their relationship.
 …one more partner feels genuinely heard and understood.
 …one more relationship blossom with trust and joy.

To make a real difference for someone else, all you have to do is… and it takes less than 60 seconds… leave a review.

Simply scan the QR code below to leave your review:

If helping another couple find their way feels good to you, then welcome to the club. You're one of us.

I'm excited to help you improve your relationship faster, easier, and more deeply than you can imagine. You'll love the exercises and strategies in the upcoming chapters.

Thank you from the bottom of my heart. Now, let's dive back into the journey toward a happier, more connected relationship.

Your biggest fan, Thomas R. Bächler

PS - Fun fact: When you give something valuable to others, it makes you even more valuable to them. If you believe this book can help someone you know, share it with them!

SIX

Navigating Life Transitions Together

H ave you ever paused to consider how life's inevitable transitions can shape your relationship? Whether it's moving to a new city, starting a family, or dealing with job changes, these transitions can be both exhilarating and daunting. They test the resilience of your relationship and often bring unexpected challenges that can strain even the strongest partnerships. One of the most common and impactful of these transitions is financial strain. It's a topic that many couples find uncomfortable to discuss, yet it's crucial for maintaining a healthy relationship.

6.1 Managing Relationship Stress During Financial Strain

Financial stress can infiltrate every corner of a relationship, triggering a range of emotional responses and behaviors. When money becomes tight, feelings of anxiety, frustration, and even shame can emerge, making it difficult for partners to communicate openly. You might find yourself snapping at each other over small expenses or feeling a constant undercurrent of tension. Financial insecurity can lead to sleepless nights, constant worry about the future, and a sense of helplessness that can erode the emotional foundation of your relationship. Understanding these impacts is the first step toward addressing them constructively.

Open and constructive communication is crucial when dealing with financial stress. Rather than avoiding the topic or letting it become a source of conflict, set aside regular times to discuss your finances. Consider establishing a "financial date" once a month where you review your budget, discuss upcoming expenses, and set financial goals together. During these discussions, approach the conversation with empathy and a non-judgmental attitude. Focus on working as a team rather than pointing fingers. For instance, instead of saying, "You're spending too much money," try expressing your concern in a more collaborative way, such as, "How can we adjust our spending to meet our savings goals?"

Creating and maintaining a joint budget is another essential strategy for managing financial stress. Start by listing all your income sources and expenses, categorizing them into needs and wants. This can help you identify areas where you can cut back without feeling deprived. Setting financial goals that reflect both partners' needs and values is crucial. Maybe one of you values saving for a future vacation while the other prioritizes paying off debt. By aligning your goals and working towards them together, you can create a sense of shared purpose and mutual support. Regularly review and adjust your budget as needed, ensuring it remains realistic and aligned with your financial situation.

Managing stress related to financial problems also involves taking care of your mental and emotional well-being. Mindfulness exercises, such as deep breathing or meditation, can help you stay grounded and reduce anxiety. Even just a few minutes of mindful breathing each day can make a significant difference in your stress levels. If the financial issues are particularly complex or overwhelming, seeking professional financial advice can provide clarity and guidance. A financial advisor can help you create a plan to manage debt, build savings, and secure your financial future. Additionally, finding low-cost ways to enjoy time together can alleviate some of the emotional strain. Simple activities like cooking a meal at home, going for a walk, or having a movie night can provide joy and connection without adding financial stress.

<hr>

Interactive Exercise: Creating a Financial Vision Board

To make financial planning more engaging, consider creating a financial vision board together. Gather magazines and printouts or draw representations of your financial goals, such as a picture of a dream vacation, a new home, or a debt-free future. Spend an evening cutting out images and arranging them on a board. This visual representation can serve as a daily reminder of what you are working towards and keep you motivated during challenging times.

Understanding the impacts of financial stress and employing these strategies can help you navigate tough financial periods. By fostering open communication, creating and maintaining a budget, and taking care of your mental well-being, you can manage financial stress together, building a stronger and more resilient relationship.

6.2 Transitioning to Parenthood: Keeping the Connection

The arrival of a new baby brings immense joy, but it also demands significant adjustments. Preparing for parenthood involves more than just setting up a nursery or buying baby clothes. Emotionally, it's vital to discuss your expectations, fears, and hopes for this new chapter. Open conversations about parenting styles, division of labor, and how life will change can help align your expectations. On a practical level, creating a schedule for baby care tasks, like feeding and diaper changes, can also alleviate stress. Attending prenatal classes together can provide both knowledge and a shared experience, reinforcing your partnership as you step into this new role.

Infertility can bring its own set of emotional and relational challenges. The struggle to conceive often leads to feelings of inadequacy, guilt, shame, and emotional distance. Supporting each other through this difficult time is crucial. Open communication about your feelings, fears, and disappointments can prevent misunderstandings and feelings of isolation. It's important to remember that it's okay to seek professional help. Infertility treatments can be physically and emotionally taxing, and a therapist specializing in fertility issues can offer support and coping strategies. Additionally, joining support groups where you can share experiences with others facing similar challenges can provide comfort and reduce feelings of isolation.

Once the baby arrives, maintaining emotional and physical intimacy can become challenging but remains crucial for relationship satisfaction. The demands of a newborn can leave both partners feeling exhausted and overwhelmed, often pushing intimacy to the back burner. To keep the connection alive, prioritize small gestures of affection, like a quick hug, a kiss, or holding hands. Finding time for uninterrupted conversations, even if it's just a few minutes while the baby naps, can help maintain emotional closeness. For physical intimacy, communicate openly about your needs and any concerns, and be patient with each other as you navigate this new phase. Scheduling regular date nights, even if they're at home, can also help keep the romance alive.

Balancing the roles of being partners and parents requires intentional effort. It's easy to let the demands of parenting overshadow your relationship, but setting aside time just for the two of you is essential. Establishing a routine where you can have regular couple time, whether it's a weekly date night or a daily check-in, can help maintain your connection. Sharing parenting responsibilities equally can also prevent one partner from feeling overwhelmed or resentful. Discussing and agreeing on how to divide tasks like feeding, diaper changes, and night shifts can ensure that both partners feel supported and valued. Remember, teamwork is key, and maintaining a sense of partnership in parenting can strengthen your bond.

Utilizing external support systems can significantly ease the transition to parenthood and reduce the burden on your relationship. Don't hesitate to lean on family and friends for help. Whether it's asking a relative to babysit so you can have some alone time or seeking advice from experienced parents, external support can provide much-needed relief. Joining parent groups or online forums can also offer a sense of community and shared understanding. These groups can be a great resource for practical advice and emotional support, helping you feel less alone in your parenting journey. Additionally, consider hiring professional help, like a postpartum doula, if it's within your means, to assist with baby care and household tasks.

Reflection Exercise: Parenting Roles and Responsibilities

Take some time to discuss and write down the parenting roles and responsibilities you each envision. List out tasks like feeding, diaper changes, nighttime duties, and playtime. Then, discuss how you can share these responsibilities in a way that feels fair and supportive to both partners. Revisit this list periodically to make adjustments as needed, ensuring that both partners feel valued and supported.

By preparing emotionally and practically, maintaining intimacy, balancing roles, and utilizing support systems, you can navigate the transition to parenthood while keeping your relationship strong.

6.3 Career Changes and Relationship Dynamics

Career changes, whether exciting promotions, unexpected job losses, or deliberate shifts in career paths, have a profound impact on relationship dynamics. These transitions can affect everything from your daily routines to your sense of identity and power balance within the relationship. Imagine one partner landing a high-profile promotion that demands longer hours and more travel. While this achievement is worth celebrating, it can also lead to shifts in household roles and responsibilities, potentially creating feelings of imbalance or resentment. Conversely, a job loss can trigger a crisis of confidence and financial strain, placing additional emotional and practical burdens on both partners. Navigating these shifts requires a deep understanding and a shared commitment to maintaining equilibrium in the relationship.

Supporting each other through career transitions is about being present and engaged, both emotionally and practically. When one partner is dealing with the uncertainties of a job search, the other can play a critical role by being an active listener. Offering a sympathetic ear without immediately jumping in with solutions can provide much-needed emotional support. Practical help, such as reviewing resumes, practicing interview questions, or sharing job leads, can also be invaluable. Adjusting household responsibilities to accommodate the new career demands or the increased time spent job hunting is another crucial area. For instance, if one partner is working longer hours due to a new job, the other might take on more household chores temporarily. These adjustments show that you're in it together, reinforcing the partnership's strength.

Negotiating a healthy work-life balance is vital to ensure that both partners' career ambitions and the relationship's needs are respected. This balance is often easier said than done, especially when career demands are high. Start by setting clear boundaries between work and personal time. For example, establish rules like no work emails after a certain hour or dedicating weekends to family activities. Communicating openly about your work schedules and any upcoming busy periods can help manage expectations and reduce conflicts. It's also important to regularly reassess these boundaries and make adjustments as needed. Flexibility and mutual respect are key to maintaining a balance that supports both your professional goals and your relationship.

Effective communication during career stress is another cornerstone of navigating career changes. When discussing career aspirations and frustrations, it's crucial to create a safe space where both partners can express their feelings without fear of judgment. Practice active listening by focusing on what your partner is saying, reflecting back their feelings, and asking open-ended questions to encourage deeper conversation. Share your own career-related stressors openly and honestly, but be mindful of not letting these frustrations spill over into your relationship negatively. For instance, if you've had a tough day at work, instead of venting all your frustration onto your partner, take a moment to decompress first. Then, share your experiences in a way that invites empathy and support rather than escalating tension.

To navigate these conversations effectively, consider setting aside a specific time each week to discuss career-related topics. However, some moments require more immediate attention. Asking your partner, "Do you have the emotional and mental bandwidth to listen to me vent for a few minutes?" can go a long way. This dedicated space can help contain work-related stress, ensuring it doesn't overshadow other aspects of your relationship. During these discussions, use "I" statements to express your feelings and needs, such as "I feel stressed about the upcoming project deadline and could use some extra support this week." This approach minimizes blame and focuses on your personal experiences, making it easier for your partner to respond with empathy and understanding.

Career transitions are inevitable, and their impact on relationship dynamics can be significant. By supporting each other emotionally and practically, negotiating a healthy work-life balance, and communicating effectively during times of career stress, you can navigate these changes together. This approach mitigates the potential negative effects and strengthens your bond, reinforcing the partnership's resilience in the face of life's many challenges.

6.4 Aging Together: Adapting to New Life Phases

As we age, both our bodies and minds undergo significant changes that can impact our relationship dynamics. Physically, you might notice shifts in energy levels, mobility, or health conditions that require more attention and care. Psychologically, the process of aging can bring about reflections on life achievements, unfulfilled dreams, and sometimes even a sense of loss or anxiety about the future. Embracing these changes positively involves acknowledging them openly with your partner and finding proactive ways to adapt. Discussing how you both feel about aging, sharing your fears and hopes, and planning together can foster a sense of unity and resilience. It's about viewing these changes as new chapters rather than endings, focusing on the opportunities they bring for growth and deeper connection.

Maintaining physical and emotional intimacy in later life often comes with its own set of challenges and misconceptions. There's a common, though misguided, belief that intimacy wanes with age, but this doesn't have to be the case. Physical intimacy may require adjustments due to health issues or changes in physical capabilities, but it can remain a fulfilling part of your relationship. Open communication about your needs and any discomforts is crucial. Experimenting with different forms of physical affection, such as gentle massages, cuddling, or simply holding hands, can keep the physical connection strong. Emotional intimacy, on the other hand, deepens as you share more life experiences together. Continue to engage in meaningful conversations, share your thoughts and feelings regularly, and make time for activities that you both enjoy. These efforts can help sustain a rich emotional bond.

Planning for retirement is a significant milestone that can drastically change your lifestyle and relationship dynamics. While financial planning is a critical component, the topic is robust. Start by discussing your vision for retirement with your partner. Do you both want to travel, volunteer, spend more time with family, or pursue hobbies? Aligning your goals can prevent potential conflicts and ensure a harmonious transition. Financially, work together to create a retirement plan that covers your needs and aspirations. This might involve meeting with a financial advisor to ensure you're on the right track. Beyond finances, consider how you'll spend your days and maintain a sense of purpose. Establishing routines and finding new activities to enjoy together can make this phase of life both exciting and fulfilling.

Supporting each other through health challenges is another vital aspect of aging together. Health issues can arise unexpectedly, and being prepared to support one another can alleviate the emotional and physical toll. Empathy and patience are key. Understand that health challenges can be frustrating and scary for both partners, and it's important to approach these situations with compassion. Shared decision-making is crucial when it comes to medical treatments or lifestyle changes. Ensure that both partners feel involved and respected in these decisions. This might involve attending doctors' appointments together, discussing treatment options openly, and making joint decisions about care plans. Maintaining open lines of communication about how you're each coping can also provide emotional support and strengthen your bond.

In navigating these later life phases, remember that adaptability and mutual support are your greatest assets. Embrace the changes together, maintain intimacy, plan for retirement thoughtfully, and support each other through health challenges. These efforts will not only help you adapt to the new phases of life but also deepen your connection and strengthen your relationship for the years to come.

SEVEN

Personal Growth for Relationship Health

Have you ever felt drained and wondered how it affects your relationship? Imagine trying to pour from an empty cup; it's simply not possible. This analogy perfectly captures the importance of self-care in maintaining the health of your relationship. Self-care isn't just about pampering yourself with spa days or indulgent treats —though those can be part of it—it's about taking deliberate actions to nurture your physical, emotional, and mental well-being. By doing so, you ensure that you have the energy, patience, and emotional bandwidth to invest in your relationship.

7.1 The Role of Personal Self-Care in Relationships

Understanding self-care begins with recognizing its multifaceted nature. Physical self-care includes activities that maintain your physical health, such as regular exercise, balanced nutrition, and adequate sleep. These basic elements might seem mundane, but they lay the groundwork for your overall well-being. Emotional self-care, on the other hand, involves activities that help you process and express your feelings, such as talking to a friend, journaling, or engaging in creative hobbies. Mental self-care focuses on activities that stimulate your mind and reduce stress, like reading, meditating, or practicing mindfulness.

When you prioritize self-care, you benefit both you and your relationship. Proper self-care prevents resentment by reducing emotional dependency on your partner. When you're emotionally and mentally balanced, you're less likely to offload your stress onto your partner or expect them to fulfill your every emotional need. This fosters a healthier dynamic where both partners are responsible for their own well-being, creating a more balanced and supportive relationship. For example, if you're taking care of your emotional health through regular therapy sessions or mindfulness practices, you're better equipped to handle relationship challenges without becoming overwhelmed or overly dependent on your partner for emotional support.

Incorporating self-care into your routine doesn't have to be overwhelming. Start with small, manageable changes that fit your lifestyle. If you're a busy professional, find ways to integrate physical activity into your day, like taking the stairs instead of the elevator or doing a quick workout during lunch. Ensure you're getting enough rest by setting a regular sleep schedule and creating a calming bedtime routine. Emotional self-care can be as simple as setting aside 10 minutes each day to reflect on your feelings through journaling or engaging in a hobby that brings you joy. Mental self-care might involve setting boundaries around your work hours to prevent burnout or scheduling regular breaks to recharge.

Supporting each other's self-care efforts is a crucial aspect of a healthy relationship. This involves understanding and respecting your partner's need for personal time and space. For instance, if your partner enjoys reading as a form of mental self-care, give them the uninterrupted time they need to immerse themselves in a book. Sharing responsibilities is another way to support each other's self-care. If one partner is feeling overwhelmed with household chores, offer to take over some of those tasks to free up time for their self-care activities. This mutual support strengthens your bond and ensures that both partners have the opportunity to recharge and maintain their well-being.

Interactive Exercise: Self-Care Check-In

Take a moment to sit down with your partner and discuss your current self-care routines. Use the following prompts to guide your conversation:

1. What activities do you currently do for physical self-care?
2. How do you take care of your emotional well-being?
3. What mental self-care practices do you find effective?
4. Are there any self-care activities you'd like to try but haven't yet?
5. How can we support each other in our self-care efforts?

After discussing these questions, create a plan together to incorporate your desired self-care activities into your daily routines. Consider setting up reminders or scheduling specific times for these activities to ensure they become a regular part of your lives. By actively engaging in this exercise, you'll not only enhance your individual well-being but also strengthen your relationship through mutual support and understanding.

7.2 Managing Uneven Investment in Relationship Work

Have you ever felt like you're the only one putting in the effort to improve your relationship? It's a common scenario where one partner seems more invested in the relationship work than the other. This discrepancy often stems from varied perspectives, experiences, and levels of comfort with therapy and self-help. While one partner might be eager to dive into relationship exercises and discussions, the other might feel overwhelmed, intimidated, or unsure about the process. It's crucial to respect each other's transition preparedness. Understanding that each person has their own pace and comfort level can reduce frustration and foster a more supportive environment. By acknowledging these differences, you create a space where both partners feel valued and understood, even if their levels of investment vary.

Shadow work is a powerful tool for personal growth that can help address this imbalance. Shadow work involves going inward to confront and resolve unresolved concerns and projections. Often, when we focus solely on our partner's need for change, we overlook our own areas that require attention. For instance, if you find yourself frequently frustrated with your partner for not engaging in relationship work, it might be worth examining your own fears or insecurities. Shadow work encourages you to recognize these internal issues and work on them, setting an example for your partner. True transformation comes from within, and by focusing on your own growth, you can inspire your partner without even trying. This process of self-discovery and healing can lead to a more balanced and harmonious relationship as both partners take responsibility for their own growth.

Encouraging a less invested partner to participate more in relationship work requires a gentle and patient approach. Start with short, non-intimidating exercises that are easy to integrate into daily life. For example, you might begin with a simple gratitude exercise where you both share one thing you appreciate about each other each day. Emphasizing the benefits of the workbook can also be motivating. Explain how these exercises can lead to a deeper connection, better communication, and increased happiness in the relationship. Instead of making demands, extend invitations. For instance, say, "I found this interesting exercise in our workbook. Would you like to try it with me?" This approach makes participation feel like a choice rather than an obligation, increasing the likelihood of engagement.

Creating a supportive environment is essential for encouraging both partners to invest in relationship work. This involves making each partner feel safe and supported in their efforts. Promote collaboration by emphasizing empathy, patience, and open communication. For example, if your partner expresses hesitation about a particular exercise, listen to their concerns without judgment and discuss how you can adjust the activity to make it more comfortable for both of you. It's also important to recognize that a partner may feel ready to dive into an exercise but then become overwhelmed once they begin. If this happens, encourage open communication and reassure them that it's okay to step away or reset. Flexibility is key—taking a break or adjusting the pace can prevent frustration and keep the process positive. Celebrating small wins and progress is another way to keep both partners motivated and engaged. Acknowledge and appreciate each other's efforts, no matter how small. This positive reinforcement can build momentum and encourage continued participation. For instance, if your partner makes an effort to engage in a new exercise, express your appreciation and highlight the positive impact it has on your relationship.

Reflection Exercise: Balance Journal

Start a "Balance Journal" where you each note down your contributions to relationship work. This could include activities like completing workbook exercises, initiating meaningful conversations, or even small gestures of kindness. At the end of each week, review your entries together and discuss how you can support each other better. This exercise can help both partners recognize their efforts and identify areas where they can contribute more equally.

By focusing on these strategies, you create a balanced and supportive environment where both partners feel valued and motivated to invest in their relationship. This chapter is just one step in a broader journey towards personal growth and relationship health, providing you with the tools and insights needed to navigate the complexities of uneven investment in relationship work.

7.3 Developing Personal Goals That Support Your Partnership

Aligning personal and relationship goals can be a delicate dance, but it's one that can significantly enhance both individual and mutual satisfaction. Imagine sitting down with your partner to discuss your aspirations, from career ambitions to personal hobbies, and finding ways to integrate these into your relationship goals. This process starts with open communication. Share your personal dreams and listen attentively as your partner shares theirs. For instance, if you aspire to advance in your career, discuss how this might affect your time together and what adjustments might be necessary. Conversely, if your partner dreams of traveling more, consider how you can plan trips that also align with your work schedule. The aim is to find intersections where your personal growth supports your relationship, creating a synergy that benefits both partners.

Setting S.M.A.R.T. goals is a practical way to ensure that your personal aspirations and relationship objectives are clear and achievable. S.M.A.R.T stands for Specific, Measurable, Achievable, Relevant, and Time-bound. Let's break this down with an example. Suppose you want to improve your physical fitness while also spending more quality time with your partner. A S.M.A.R.T goal could be: "We will go for a 30-minute walk together three times a week for the next three months." This goal is specific (30-minute walks), measurable (three times a week), achievable (fits into your schedule), relevant (improves fitness and quality time), and time-bound (three months). By setting such goals, you create a clear roadmap that guides both your personal and relationship growth, ensuring that your individual achievements contribute to your partnership's well-being.

Personal achievements can significantly boost self-esteem and confidence, which in turn invigorates the relationship with positive energy and inspiration. When you accomplish a personal goal, whether it's completing a course, running a marathon, or mastering a new skill, you bring that sense of fulfillment and self-assurance into your relationship. This positive energy can be contagious, inspiring your partner to pursue their own goals and creating a cycle of mutual encouragement and growth. Imagine the pride and joy you feel when your partner celebrates your achievements with you and vice versa. This shared celebration strengthens your bond and reinforces the idea that your individual successes are integral to your collective happiness.

However, there are times when personal goals may conflict, requiring negotiation and compromise to ensure that both partners feel supported. For instance, if one partner wants to pursue a demanding career that requires long hours while the other dreams of starting a family soon, these goals might initially seem at odds. It's crucial to approach such situations with empathy and a willingness to find common ground. Start by discussing the underlying motivations for each goal and explore possible compromises. Perhaps the partner with career ambitions can set a timeline for achieving certain milestones before starting a family, or the couple can agree on a plan that balances both career growth and family life. The key is to ensure that both partners feel heard and that their needs are addressed, creating a collaborative approach to achieving both personal and relationship goals.

Navigating conflicting goals requires patience and open-mindedness. It's about understanding that both partners' aspirations are valid and finding ways to support each other's dreams without sacrificing your own. For example, if one partner's goal is to go back to school, discuss how this might affect your daily routines and how you can support each other during this period. Maybe the other partner can take on more household responsibilities or adjust their work schedule to accommodate study time. By working together and being flexible, you can create a supportive environment where both partners can pursue their individual goals while also strengthening their relationship.

Reflection Exercise: Goal Alignment Chart

Create a Goal Alignment Chart where you list your individual goals and relationship goals. Discuss how each personal goal can support or align with your relationship objectives. Use this chart to identify potential conflicts and brainstorm ways to address them. This exercise will help you visualize how your personal growth can enhance your partnership and provide a clear plan for achieving your goals together.

7.4 Self-Reflection and Its Impact on Relationships

Have you ever found yourself reacting to your partner in ways that seem out of proportion to the situation? Regular self-reflection can be a powerful tool in understanding these reactions. By taking the time to look inward, you uncover the motivations, desires, and behaviors that shape your interactions. This awareness can lead to healthier relationship dynamics by allowing you to recognize patterns and triggers that might otherwise go unnoticed. For instance, if you notice that you often become defensive during discussions about finances, self-reflection might reveal underlying anxieties about financial security rooted in past experiences. Understanding these triggers helps you approach such conversations with more empathy and less reactivity, fostering a more harmonious relationship.

Effective self-reflection can be achieved through various methods, each offering unique benefits. Journaling is a straightforward yet profound way to process your thoughts and emotions. By writing down your feelings and experiences, you create a tangible record that can help you identify patterns and gain insights. Meditation offers another path, allowing you to quiet the mind and observe your thoughts without judgment. This practice can increase your awareness of your emotional landscape, making it easier to manage stress and maintain emotional balance. Therapy provides a structured environment for deep self-exploration, guided by a professional who can offer objective insights and strategies for personal growth. Engaging in these practices regularly can significantly enhance your self-awareness, equipping you with the tools to navigate your relationship with greater clarity and understanding.

The insights gained from self-reflection can profoundly impact your relationship. When you understand your motivations and reactions, you can communicate more clearly with your partner. Imagine a scenario where you often feel neglected when your partner spends time on their hobbies. Through self-reflection, you might realize that this feeling stems from a need for more quality time together. Armed with this insight, you can express your needs more effectively, saying something like, "I value our time together and would love to set aside specific evenings for us to connect." This clarity not only helps your partner understand your perspective but also makes it easier to find mutually satisfying solutions. Additionally, self-reflection enables you to make better decisions within your relationship, as it grounds your choices in a deeper understanding of your needs and values.

Creating a culture of openness and growth within your relationship further amplifies the benefits of self-reflection. When both partners feel safe to share their reflections and growth experiences, it fosters an environment of mutual development. Encourage open dialogues where you both discuss your self-reflection practices and the insights you've gained. For example, you might set aside time each week to share your reflections, discussing how they relate to your relationship and exploring ways to support each other's growth. This practice strengthens your bond and creates a dynamic where both partners feel valued and understood. By normalizing these conversations, you build a foundation of trust and transparency, making it easier to navigate challenges and celebrate successes together.

In nurturing this culture of openness, it's essential to approach these conversations with empathy and non-judgment. Actively listen to your partner's reflections, validate their feelings, and offer support without trying to fix or change them. This creates a safe space where both partners can explore their inner worlds without fear of criticism. Celebrating each other's growth milestones, no matter how small, reinforces the positive impact of self-reflection and encourages continued personal development. Over time, this culture of openness and growth becomes a cornerstone of your relationship, enhancing your emotional connection and resilience.

Reflection Exercise: Self-Reflection Journal Prompts

Consider starting a self-reflection journal with prompts like:

1. What emotions did I feel most strongly this week, and what triggered them?
2. How did I respond to my partner during moments of conflict, and why?
3. What personal needs or desires did I overlook, and how can I address them?
4. In what ways did I support my partner's growth, and how can I improve?

By regularly engaging with these prompts, you can deepen your self-awareness and bring greater clarity to your relationship interactions.

As you integrate self-reflection into your daily routine and foster a culture of openness and growth within your relationship, you'll find that your interactions become more meaningful and your bond stronger. This chapter has explored the transformative power of self-reflection, offering practical strategies and insights to enhance your relationship. Looking ahead, we will delve into the dynamics of culturally informed relationship practices, guiding you through the complexities of navigating cultural differences within your partnership.

EIGHT

Culturally Informed Relationship Dynamics

H ave you ever found yourself puzzled by your partner's family traditions or communication style, wondering how to bridge that gap? Cultural differences can be both enriching and challenging in a relationship. They shape who we are and how we interact with the world, influencing our values, traditions, communication styles, and social behaviors. When two people come together from different cultural backgrounds, it's like blending two unique tapestries into a new, vibrant pattern.

8.1 Understanding and Respecting Cultural Differences

Cultural identity is a fascinating and complex mosaic composed of various elements that define who we are. Values are at the core of this identity, reflecting what we hold dear and guiding our decisions and actions. For example, some cultures place a high value on collectivism, emphasizing family and community bonds, while others prioritize individualism and personal achievements. These differing values can influence how partners approach everything from career choices to family responsibilities.

Traditions also play a significant role in shaping cultural identity. These are the rituals and customs passed down through generations, often tied to important life events like weddings, holidays, and family gatherings. Imagine one partner coming from a culture where extended family gatherings are frequent and expected, while the other's background involves more intimate, nuclear family events. Navigating these differences requires understanding and compromise to ensure both partners feel respected and included.

Communication styles are another critical component of cultural identity. They can vary widely, from direct and assertive to indirect and subtle. In some cultures, expressing disagreement openly is seen as honest and constructive, while in others, it might be considered disrespectful or confrontational. Recognizing these differences can prevent misunderstandings and help partners communicate more effectively. Social behaviors, including how we interact with friends, colleagues, and strangers, are also influenced by our cultural backgrounds. These behaviors encompass everything from greeting customs to conflict resolution strategies.

Navigating cultural differences can be challenging, and couples often face several common hurdles. Differing family dynamics are a frequent source of tension. For instance, one partner might come from a family where elders are highly respected and consulted for major decisions, while the other's family operates more democratically, with each member having an equal say. These differing expectations can lead to conflicts if not addressed openly and respectfully. Dietary habits can also pose challenges. Cultural backgrounds often influence our food preferences and restrictions, which can become a point of contention if not handled with understanding and flexibility. Imagine one partner adhering to a vegetarian diet due to cultural or religious reasons while the other enjoys a diet that includes meat. Finding a balance that respects both partners' choices is crucial.

Expectations about roles within the relationship are another area where cultural differences can create friction. In some cultures, traditional gender roles are more pronounced, with clear expectations about who handles which responsibilities. In others, roles might be more fluid and shared. These differing expectations can lead to misunderstandings and resentment if not discussed and negotiated openly.

Adapting to and respecting cultural differences without losing one's identity requires active effort and open communication. It begins with a genuine interest in learning about each other's culture. This could involve reading books, watching documentaries, or participating in cultural events together. The aim is to develop a deeper understanding of the values, traditions, and practices that shape your partner's worldview. Open communication about cultural practices is also essential. Discussing how each of you was raised, what traditions are important to you, and how you'd like to incorporate these into your shared life can help bridge gaps and foster mutual respect. It's about finding common ground where both partners feel valued and respected.

This involves creating new, shared traditions that blend elements from both cultures. This could be as simple as combining food traditions from both backgrounds in your meals or celebrating holidays from both cultures. The goal is to create a shared cultural identity that honors both partners' backgrounds while forging new, meaningful experiences together.

Embracing cultural diversity brings numerous benefits to a relationship. It broadens perspectives, allowing both partners to see the world through a different lens. This can lead to richer, more varied experiences and a stronger, more resilient bond. When you embrace each other's cultures, you add variety to your life, and you build a deeper understanding and appreciation for each other..

⸻

Reflection Exercise: Cultural Exploration Journal

Start a cultural exploration journal together. Dedicate time each week to learning about each other's cultural backgrounds. Write down your findings, reflections, and any new traditions you create together. This can be a fun and enlightening way to deepen your understanding and appreciation of each other's cultures while building a shared cultural identity.

8.2 Navigating Interfaith Relationships

Navigating interfaith relationships can be incredibly rewarding but also brings its own set of challenges. Different religious beliefs can profoundly impact various aspects of a relationship, including celebrations, dietary restrictions, moral decisions, and child-rearing. Imagine the complexities that arise when one partner is committed to attending weekly religious services while the other is not or when dietary restrictions due to religious beliefs mean separate meals must be prepared. These differences can manifest in numerous ways, from the foods you eat to the values you teach your children and even the ways you celebrate holidays and milestones. Understanding the impact of these differing beliefs is crucial for creating a harmonious relationship.

Celebrations are a significant area where religious differences become evident. For instance, one partner might celebrate Christmas with great enthusiasm while the other observes Hanukkah, leading to potential conflicts about which holidays to prioritize. These differing traditions can sometimes make partners feel isolated or misunderstood if not approached with sensitivity and respect. Dietary restrictions are another key aspect influenced by religious beliefs. One partner might follow a kosher or halal diet, while the other does not, requiring careful consideration and planning for meals. Moral decisions, often guided by religious teachings, can also differ. Consider decisions about charitable giving, ethical business practices, or even daily behaviors like dressing modestly or observing a day of rest. These choices reflect deeper values and can lead to disagreements if not discussed openly. Child-rearing is perhaps the most delicate area impacted by religious differences. Deciding how to raise children, which religious teachings to impart, and how to celebrate religious milestones can be a source of tension if not navigated thoughtfully.

Communicating about faith openly and respectfully is vital in interfaith relationships. It's not about convincing or changing each other's views but understanding and respecting them. Start by creating a safe space where both partners feel comfortable sharing their beliefs, practices, and the importance of these to their identity. This dialogue should be ongoing, not a one-time conversation. Encourage each other to ask questions and express genuine curiosity about each other's faith. For example, instead of saying, "Why do you have to fast during Ramadan?" you might ask, "Can you share what fasting during Ramadan means to you and how it impacts your day?" This approach encourages understanding without judgment.

Respecting religious practices means supporting each other's faith activities without compromising your own beliefs. This could involve attending religious services together or apart, participating in each other's religious rituals occasionally, or simply acknowledging and respecting each other's need for solitude or communal worship. For instance, if your partner needs to pray at specific times during the day, find ways to support this practice without feeling excluded. Maybe this means scheduling activities around these times or creating a quiet space in your home for prayer. These small acts of respect can significantly strengthen your bond and show your partner that you value their spiritual needs.

Handling religious celebrations and rituals requires creativity and flexibility. Instead of viewing these occasions as points of contention, see them as opportunities to create new, inclusive traditions that honor both faiths.

For example, during the holiday season, you might celebrate both Christmas and Hanukkah by incorporating elements of each into your home décor and festivities. Create a shared calendar of religious holidays and plan how to observe each one together, ensuring that both partners feel their traditions are valued. If you have children, this approach can also teach them the importance of respecting and celebrating diversity. You might even create new family traditions that blend elements from both faiths, such as a special meal or ritual that incorporates the values and practices of each religion.

Navigating interfaith relationships also involves understanding the deeper values and teachings behind religious practices. This understanding can help you find common ground and shared values that transcend specific religious doctrines. For instance, many religions emphasize principles like compassion, honesty, and charity. By focusing on these shared values, you can create a strong moral foundation for your relationship, even if the specific practices differ. Engaging in interfaith dialogue groups or workshops can also provide valuable insights and support from others in similar situations. These platforms offer a space to share experiences, challenges, and strategies for navigating interfaith dynamics.

Supporting each other in interfaith relationships means being present and engaged in each other's spiritual journeys. This support can take many forms, from attending services together to discussing religious texts and their relevance to your lives. It's about showing genuine interest and respect for each other's beliefs and finding ways to integrate them into your shared life. For example, you might set aside time each week to discuss religious teaching and how it applies to your relationship or daily life. This practice can deepen your understanding of each other's faith and create a shared spiritual space that strengthens your bond.

In navigating interfaith relationships, the key is to approach each other's beliefs with curiosity, respect, and a willingness to learn. By understanding the impact of differing religious beliefs on various aspects of your relationship, communicating openly and respectfully about faith, respecting each other's practices, and finding inclusive ways to celebrate religious rituals, you can create a harmonious and enriching partnership. This journey requires ongoing effort and a commitment to mutual respect, but the rewards of a deeper, more nuanced connection are well worth it.

8.3 Celebrating Diverse Traditions Together

Creating shared cultural experiences can be one of the most rewarding aspects of a multicultural relationship. Imagine the richness of blending elements from both partners' backgrounds to form new traditions that are uniquely yours. This isn't about replacing your individual traditions but rather weaving them together to create something that reflects both of your identities. For instance, you might decide to celebrate a holiday from each culture, incorporating foods, music, and customs from both backgrounds. This honors your individual heritage and also supports a shared cultural identity within your relationship. It's a beautiful way to demonstrate mutual respect and love, creating memories that both of you will cherish.

Educational family activities are another fantastic way to celebrate diverse traditions. These activities can be particularly beneficial if you have children, as they help promote a sense of unity and appreciation for diversity from a young age. Consider setting aside time each month to explore a different aspect of each culture. This could involve cooking traditional dishes together, learning a folk dance, or reading stories from your respective backgrounds. For example, one month, you might focus on traditional crafts from one culture, while the next month, you delve into the historical landmarks of the other. These activities educate and create bonding opportunities for the whole family.

Involving extended family members in your cultural exchanges and celebrations can significantly enhance these experiences. It's not uncommon for extended family members to feel left out or unsure about how to engage with the other culture. Invite them to join by explaining the significance of certain traditions and encouraging their participation. This could mean inviting both sides of the family to a joint cultural celebration or organizing a family gathering where everyone brings a dish from their cultural background. Such events can help build bridges and deepen mutual familial respect. For instance, if one family celebrates Diwali and the other Christmas, you could host a combined celebration where both traditions are honored. This enriches the experience and creates a sense of inclusion and belonging among all family members.

Documenting and sharing your cultural journey can be a powerful way to reflect on and celebrate your relationship's diversity. Consider starting a blog or social media account dedicated to your experiences, where you can share stories, photos, and insights about your cultural integration. This can serve as a testament to your commitment to embracing diversity and can also inspire others in similar situations. Alternatively, you might prefer to keep a private family album filled with photos and notes about your shared cultural experiences. This can be a cherished keepsake, something you can look back on together and even pass down to future generations. Documenting your journey allows you to see how far you've come and reinforces the value of the efforts you've made to understand and integrate each other's cultures.

Creating shared cultural experiences, engaging in educational family activities, involving extended family members, and documenting your journey are all ways to celebrate and honor the diversity within your relationship. By actively embracing and celebrating your cultural differences, you build a stronger, more resilient relationship that can navigate the complexities of the multicultural world we live in.

NINE

The Role of Technology in Modern Relationships

H ave you ever caught yourself scrolling through social media, only to realize that hours have slipped away without even noticing? In today's digital age, technology is deeply woven into the fabric of our daily lives, influencing how we connect, communicate, and even perceive our relationships. While technology offers countless benefits, from staying connected with loved ones to discovering new interests, it also brings its own set of challenges. These challenges can manifest in various ways, particularly when it comes to social media and the boundaries we set—or fail to set—within our relationships.

9.1 Social Media and Relationship Boundaries

Setting healthy social media boundaries is crucial for maintaining balance and trust in a relationship. Without mutual understanding and agreement, social media can become a breeding ground for misunderstandings, jealousy, and even conflicts. One vital aspect of setting these boundaries involves discussing what is appropriate to share about your relationship online. For some couples, posting pictures and updates about their life together might be a way to celebrate their bond. For others, such posts might feel invasive or unnecessary. It's essential to find a middle ground where both partners feel respected and comfortable. This could involve agreeing on what types of photos to share, how frequently to post about your relationship, and ensuring that both partners have a say in these decisions.

Another important boundary to consider is the issue of friending exes on social media. While some people might be comfortable staying connected with their past relationships, others might find it unsettling or even threatening. Openly discussing your feelings about this can help prevent potential misunderstandings and ensure that both partners feel secure. If one partner feels uncomfortable with the other maintaining social media connections with an ex, it's crucial to address these concerns with empathy and understanding rather than dismissing them as irrational. Setting clear guidelines on this matter can help maintain trust and prevent unnecessary conflicts.

Balancing privacy with transparency in the context of social media can be a delicate act. On one hand, maintaining a certain level of privacy is important for protecting the intimacy and uniqueness of your relationship. On the other hand, being transparent about your online activities can build trust and reduce insecurities. Couples should decide together what aspects of their online lives they are comfortable sharing with each other and what should remain private. Transparency doesn't mean sharing every detail but rather being open about your general social media habits and interactions. For example, if you enjoy engaging in online forums or groups, let your partner know about these interests. This openness can foster a sense of trust and reduce the likelihood of misunderstandings.

The impact of social media on relationship security cannot be over-stated. Social media platforms often create opportunities for interactions with others, some of which might be perceived as threats to the relation-ship. Whether it's liking a photo, commenting on a post, or private messag-ing, these interactions can sometimes lead to feelings of jealousy or insecurity. To mitigate these insecurities, it's important to establish clear communication and reassurance within the relationship. Regularly affirming your commitment and discussing any concerns openly can help build a strong foundation of trust. Additionally, being mindful of your interactions with others online and considering how they might be perceived by your partner can go a long way in maintaining relationship security.

Creating a social media agreement is a proactive step that can help couples navigate the complexities of their online interactions. This agree-ment should respect both partners' comfort levels and detail what is encouraged and what is off-limits on social networks. Start by discussing your expectations and boundaries regarding social media use. This might include agreeing on the types of content you're both comfortable sharing, the amount of time spent on social platforms, and how to handle interactions with exes or new friends. Write down these agreements and review them periodically to ensure they remain relevant and effective as your relationship evolves. This practice sets clear boundaries and reinforces mutual respect and understanding.

Interactive Element: Social Media Agreement Template

Create your own Social Media Agreement by discussing and filling out the following points:

TYPES OF CONTENT TO SHARE:

- Photos of us together: Yes/No
- Personal updates about our relationship: Yes/No
- Tagging each other in posts: Yes/No
- Sharing milestones (e.g., anniversaries): Yes/No

INTERACTIONS WITH OTHERS:

- Friending exes: Yes/No
- Liking/commenting on posts from others: Yes/No
- Messaging friends outside the relationship: Yes/No

PRIVACY AND TRANSPARENCY:

- Sharing social media passwords: Yes/No
- Informing each other about new social media accounts: Yes/No

Time Spent on Social Media:

- Maximum daily/weekly time: _____
- No social media during specific times (e.g., dinner): Yes/No

Review and Revisit:

- Schedule regular check-ins to discuss and adjust the agreement as needed.

By proactively addressing these elements, you can create a balanced and respectful approach to social media use within your relationship. This agreement serves as a living document, adaptable to the changing dynamics of your partnership and the evolving landscape of social media.

9.2 Digital Communication: Benefits and Pitfalls

In our fast-paced world, digital communication tools like texting, emailing, and video calls have become indispensable for staying connected, especially for busy couples or those separated by distance. These tools offer the convenience of instant communication, allowing you to share moments, thoughts, and feelings in real-time, regardless of where you are. These digital touchpoints can keep the emotional connection alive, providing much-needed reassurance and intimacy.

However, digital communication is not without its pitfalls. One of the most common issues is the potential for miscommunication. Tone and intent, which are easily conveyed through body language and facial expressions in face-to-face interactions, can be easily misconstrued in texts or emails. A simple message like "We need to talk" can be interpreted in multiple ways depending on the recipient's mood or assumptions. To mitigate these misunderstandings, consider using emojis or clear, explicit language to convey your emotions more accurately. For instance, adding a smiley face or stating, "I'm not upset, just want to chat," can help clarify your intent. Additionally, taking a moment to re-read your messages before sending them can ensure that your words align with your intended tone.

While digital communication offers convenience, relying too heavily on it for serious conversations can be risky. It's tempting to address difficult topics through texts or emails to avoid the immediate emotional response that a face-to-face conversation might provoke. However, this can lead to more significant misunderstandings and emotional distance. Serious matters, such as discussing relationship issues, making significant decisions, or resolving conflicts, are best handled in person or, if that's not possible, through video calls. These methods allow for the nuances of tone, facial expressions, and body language, which are crucial for conveying empathy and understanding. Face-to-face interactions also provide an opportunity for immediate feedback, allowing both partners to address concerns and emotions as they arise.

Setting guidelines for digital etiquette in relationships can help ensure that digital communication complements rather than complicates your relationship. One important guideline is to establish expectations for response times. While it's unrealistic to expect immediate replies at all times, agreeing on a general timeframe for responses can prevent feelings of neglect or anxiety. For example, you might agree that unless one partner is in a meeting or otherwise occupied, a response within a few hours is reasonable. Another critical aspect of digital etiquette is how and when to use digital communication for apologies. While a text apology might be convenient, it often lacks the sincerity and depth of an in-person apology. If you need to apologize for something significant, consider doing it face-to-face or through a video call to convey your remorse genuinely.

Another guideline is to prioritize giving undivided attention during digital interactions. It's easy to fall into the habit of multitasking while texting or chatting online, but this can make your partner feel undervalued. When you're engaging in a digital conversation, try to minimize distractions and focus on the interaction. This might mean setting aside specific times for digital dates or catch-ups, ensuring that both partners are fully present. Additionally, being mindful of your partner's schedule and respecting their time can go a long way in maintaining a healthy digital communication dynamic. If your partner is busy or stressed, consider sending a thoughtful message acknowledging their situation and expressing your support rather than expecting an immediate response.

<hr>

Reflection Exercise: Digital Communication Check-In

Take some time to discuss the role of digital communication in your relationship. Reflect on the following questions together:

- How often do we rely on digital communication for significant conversations?
- Have there been instances where our messages were misunderstood? How did we resolve them?
- What are our expectations for response times, and do they align with our daily routines?
- How can we ensure that our digital interactions are meaningful and respectful?

By addressing these questions, you can develop a more intentional approach to digital communication, enhancing your connection and avoiding common pitfalls.

9.3 Using Technology to Strengthen Long-Distance Relationships

Long-distance relationships inherently pose challenges, but technology offers a lifeline that can bridge the physical gap, supporting emotional closeness despite the miles. Video calls, for instance, are more than just a way to see each other's faces—they bring the nuances of expression and tone that text messages simply can't convey. Imagine being able to share a laugh over dinner, even from different continents, or offering a comforting smile when your partner needs it most. These interactions, though digital, can significantly reinforce your emotional connection and keep the relationship vibrant and dynamic. Beyond video calls, shared online activities like gaming or watching a movie together can create shared experiences that help maintain a sense of togetherness. Engaging in a cooperative game or streaming the same film while discussing it in real time can mimic the feeling of being in the same room, encouraging a sense of unity and shared enjoyment.

Scheduling regular digital dates is another vital strategy for sustaining a long-distance relationship. These dates can be as simple or elaborate as you like, but the key is consistency and intentionality. Set aside specific times each week or month dedicated to connecting through video calls or shared activities like cooking the same meal and dining together virtually. This routine helps anchor the relationship, offering both partners something to look forward to and ensuring that regular, meaningful interactions are prioritized despite busy schedules. Whether it's a Friday night dinner date or a Sunday morning coffee chat, these moments become cherished rituals that reinforce your bond and provide stability amid the unpredictability of long-distance dynamics.

When it comes to creative uses of technology, the possibilities are endless. Sending voice notes can add a personal touch to your conversations, allowing your partner to hear the warmth in your voice even when you can't talk in real time. Sharing digital calendars is another practical tool that keeps both partners involved in each other's lives. You can sync your schedules, set reminders for important dates, and even plan virtual activities together. There are also numerous apps specifically designed for long-distance relationships, offering features like shared photo albums, countdowns to the next visit, and even games to play together. These tools help maintain a sense of daily involvement and shared experiences, making the distance feel less daunting.

Managing time zone differences can be one of the trickiest aspects of long-distance relationships, but technology can streamline this challenge as well. Begin by syncing your schedules and establishing a routine that accommodates both time zones. This might mean adjusting your sleep or work schedules slightly to ensure you have overlapping free time. Use technology to set reminders or countdowns for important dates and meetings, helping both partners stay on track despite the differing clocks. Apps that convert time zones can also be handy, ensuring that miscommunications about meeting times are minimized. Regularly reviewing and adjusting your schedules as needed can help maintain a balanced and fair distribution of quality time, ensuring that neither partner feels neglected or overwhelmed.

As we wrap up this chapter on technology in modern relationships, it's clear that while digital tools can introduce complexities, they also offer innovative ways to stay connected and nurture emotional intimacy. From setting social media boundaries to leveraging video calls and creative apps for long-distance love, technology can be a powerful ally in maintaining a healthy and fulfilling partnership. Next, we'll explore how to navigate financial planning together, ensuring that money matters strengthen rather than strain your relationship.

TEN

Financial Planning Together

H ave you ever felt the weight of financial stress bearing down on your relationship, making every conversation about money tense and fraught with anxiety? You're not alone. Money is one of the most common sources of conflict in relationships, yet it's also one of the most crucial areas where collaboration and understanding can lead to a stronger, more resilient partnership. Think about this: A recent study found that couples who regularly discuss their finances are more likely to report being happy in their relationships. This chapter aims to help you and your partner build a solid financial foundation together, starting with the basics of budgeting.

10.1 Budgeting as a Couple

Establishing a joint budgeting process is a game-changer for managing household finances. It's more than just a spreadsheet or a list of numbers —it's a tool that aligns your financial goals and expectations, fostering transparency and teamwork. Start by sitting down with your partner and gathering all sources of income and expenses. This includes salaries, freelance earnings, side hustles, and any other financial streams. Next, list out all your expenses, from the fixed ones like rent or mortgage payments and utilities to variable ones like groceries, dining out, and entertainment.

Categorizing spending can help you see where your money is going and identify areas where you might need to cut back. Common categories include housing, transportation, food, healthcare, savings, and discretionary spending. This process might feel tedious initially, but it's essential to get a comprehensive view of your financial landscape. Once you have everything laid out, set up a system that works for both partners. This could be a joint bank account for shared expenses or a method where each partner contributes a certain percentage of their income to a collective pot while keeping separate accounts for personal use.

In today's digital age, there are numerous tools and apps designed to make budgeting easier and more efficient. Apps like Mint, YNAB (You Need A Budget), and PocketGuard offer features such as real-time tracking, categorization of expenses, and goal setting. Using these digital tools can help you stay on top of your finances, providing updates and notifications that keep you informed without the need for constant manual tracking. The advantage of these apps lies in their ability to sync with your bank accounts, offering a seamless way to monitor spending and savings in real time. This transparency can reduce misunderstandings and ensure that both partners are always on the same page.

Balancing individual and joint expenses is another critical aspect of budgeting as a couple. While it's important to manage shared expenses effectively, it's equally vital to maintain a sense of personal financial freedom. Allocating 'fun money' for each partner can help achieve this balance, allowing both of you to spend on personal desires without feeling guilty or scrutinized. This approach respects individual autonomy while ensuring that the overall financial plan remains intact. For instance, you might agree that each partner gets a certain amount of discretionary money each month to spend as they wish—whether it's on hobbies, personal treats, or gifts for friends and family. This can prevent feelings of resentment and promote a healthier financial dynamic in the relationship.

Regular budget reviews and adjustments are essential to keep your financial plan relevant and effective. Life is dynamic, and so are your financial needs and circumstances. Schedule monthly or quarterly budget meetings to review your income, expenses, and savings goals. These reviews provide a structured opportunity to discuss any changes in your financial situation, such as a salary increase, unexpected expenses, or shifts in spending habits. During these meetings, ensure that both partners have an equal say in the decision-making process. Create a safe space where you can openly discuss concerns, celebrate financial wins, and plan for future goals. Constructive budget reviews can help you stay aligned, adapt to changes, and reinforce your commitment to shared financial well-being.

―

Interactive Exercise: Monthly Budget Review Checklist

1. **GATHER FINANCIAL STATEMENTS:** Collect bank statements, credit card bills, and any other financial documents for the month.
2. **REVIEW INCOME:** Check all sources of income and compare them to your expectations.
3. **ANALYZE EXPENSES:** Go through each category of spending and note any significant changes or unexpected costs.
4. **EVALUATE SAVINGS:** Look at your savings contributions and assess whether you're on track to meet your goals.
5. **DISCUSS ADJUSTMENTS:** Talk about any necessary adjustments to your budget based on your findings.
6. **SET GOALS FOR NEXT MONTH:** Agree on specific financial goals for the upcoming month, such as reducing dining out expenses or increasing savings.

By following these steps, budgeting together can transform from a source of stress into a foundation of strength for your relationship.

10.2 Financial Goals and Relationship Stability

Start by sitting down together and discussing what you both want to achieve financially. Short-term goals might include saving for a vacation, paying off a credit card, or building an emergency fund. These goals are usually achievable within a year and provide immediate gratification, reinforcing the habit of saving and planning together.

Long-term goals require a bit more foresight and planning. Think about what you want to achieve in the next five, ten, or even twenty years. Retirement planning, buying a home, or funding your children's education are common long-term goals. These goals should reflect both your individual aspirations and your shared vision for the future. It's crucial to ensure that these goals meet both partners' needs and desires, creating a balanced and fulfilling financial plan. Discussing your values openly can help you understand what is most important to each of you, whether it's financial security, freedom to travel, or the ability to support family members.

Once you've defined your financial goals, develop strategies to achieve them. Start by prioritizing your goals—decide which ones are most important and which can be put on the back burner for now. This prioritization helps you allocate your resources more effectively. For instance, you might decide that building an emergency fund is your top priority, followed by saving for a down payment on a house. Breaking down these goals into smaller, actionable steps makes them more manageable. For short-term goals, set specific monthly saving targets and track your progress. For long-term goals, consider setting annual milestones to keep you on track.

Allocating resources wisely is another crucial aspect of achieving your financial goals. This involves creating a detailed budget that accounts for all your income and expenses and then determining how much you can realistically save each month. You might need to make some sacrifices or cut back on discretionary spending to meet your saving targets. Monitoring your progress regularly can help you stay on track and make adjustments as needed. Use tools like spreadsheets or budgeting apps to keep an eye on your savings and expenses. Celebrate small victories along the way to maintain motivation and commitment to your goals.

Shared financial goals can significantly impact your relationship's health by fostering teamwork and a sense of shared purpose. Working together towards common objectives strengthens your bond and enhances mutual trust and respect. It turns financial planning from a stressful chore into a collaborative endeavor that brings you closer together. However, challenges are inevitable. Differences in spending habits, financial priorities, or risk tolerance can create friction. It's essential to address these differences openly and empathetically. Approach these discussions with a mindset of understanding and compromise, focusing on finding solutions that work for both partners.

Life is unpredictable, and your financial goals may need to adapt to significant life changes. The birth of a child, a job change, or unexpected financial setbacks like medical emergencies can derail your plans. Flexibility is key to navigating these changes without losing sight of your long-term objectives. When faced with a significant life event, revisit your financial goals and adjust them as necessary. For example, if you have a new baby, you might need to redirect funds towards childcare or education savings. If one partner loses their job, you may need to tighten your budget and temporarily shift your focus to essential expenses.

Regularly revisiting and adjusting your financial goals ensures that your planning remains relevant and supportive of your relationship. Schedule annual financial reviews where you assess your progress, celebrate achievements, and set new goals for the future. These reviews keep you aligned and motivated, reinforcing your commitment to each other and your shared financial future. By setting clear goals, developing effective strategies, and remaining flexible in the face of life's challenges, you can build a stable and fulfilling financial future together.

10.3 Handling Financial Disagreements Constructively

Financial disagreements are a common stumbling block in many relationships, often stemming from differences in spending habits, risk tolerance, and priorities regarding saving and debt. Picture this: you might be a meticulous saver, valuing the security of a robust emergency fund, while your partner prefers to spend on experiences, believing life is too short to pinch pennies. These differing philosophies can lead to tension and misunderstandings. Similarly, risk tolerance can be a significant source of conflict. One partner might be comfortable investing in high-risk, high-reward ventures, while the other prefers the stability of low-risk investments. These opposing views can make joint financial decisions challenging, requiring careful navigation to reach a consensus. Additionally, disagreements about priorities—whether to pay off debt aggressively or save for a dream vacation—can create frustration and resentment if not addressed openly and collaboratively.

To navigate these financial disagreements, effective communication is paramount. Start by expressing your concerns without assigning blame. Instead of saying, "You always spend too much," try, "I feel anxious when our spending exceeds our budget." Using "our" rather than "your" encourages a team mentality, emphasizing that both partners share responsibility for the issue and the solution. This approach can help reduce defensiveness and make it easier to work together toward a resolution. This approach focuses on your feelings rather than your partner's actions, reducing defensiveness and opening the door for a more constructive conversation. Active listening is also crucial; this involves genuinely hearing your partner's perspective without interrupting or planning your response while they speak. Reflect back what you hear to ensure understanding, such as, "If I understand correctly, you feel that we should enjoy our money now rather than just save for the future." This technique not only clarifies communication but also shows your partner that their feelings are valued.

Using collaborative language can further enhance these discussions. Phrases like "Let's find a solution together" or "How can we balance both of our needs?" promote a sense of partnership and shared responsibility. This language creates a cooperative rather than adversarial atmosphere, making it easier to reach mutually acceptable solutions. It's also helpful to schedule regular financial check-ins, where both partners come prepared to discuss their concerns and ideas in a structured, respectful manner. These meetings provide a safe space to address issues before they escalate into larger conflicts, ensuring ongoing communication and alignment.

Negotiation and compromise are fundamental to resolving financial disagreements. The goal should be to find a middle ground that respects both partners' views while maintaining overall financial health. Start by identifying the core needs and values behind each person's financial preferences. For example, if one partner values security and the other values enjoyment, look for ways to incorporate elements of both into your financial plan. You might agree to allocate a certain percentage of your income to savings while setting aside another portion for discretionary spending. This approach ensures that both partners feel heard and respected, promoting a sense of fairness and balance.

Practical methods for finding this middle ground include setting clear financial boundaries and goals. Establish spending limits for discretionary categories and agree on savings targets that align with both partners' priorities. If disagreements arise about specific purchases or investments, consider implementing a waiting period before making any final decisions. This pause allows both partners to reflect and discuss the matter calmly, reducing the likelihood of impulsive or emotionally charged decisions. Another strategy is to create a "fun fund" for each partner, a small, agreed-upon amount that can be spent freely without needing approval from the other. This can help satisfy the desire for personal spending autonomy while keeping overall finances on track.

Sometimes, despite your best efforts, financial disagreements may persist or become too complex to handle on your own. In such cases, seeking professional help can be a wise decision. Financial advisors or counselors can provide objective, expert guidance tailored to your specific situation. They can help you develop a comprehensive financial plan, mediate discussions, and offer strategies to manage conflicts. If your disagreements are rooted in deeper emotional or relational issues, a couples therapist with experience in financial matters can also be invaluable. They can help you explore the underlying emotions and patterns driving your financial conflicts, encouraging a deeper understanding and more effective communication.

When seeking professional help, it's essential to approach it as a team. Discuss with your partner why you believe professional guidance could be beneficial and ensure they are on board with the idea. Research potential advisors or counselors together, looking for professionals with a track record of helping couples navigate financial issues. During your sessions, be open and honest about your concerns and goals, and be willing to listen to your partner's perspective. Professional advice can provide the tools and insights needed to transform your financial disagreements into opportunities for growth and collaboration.

In summary, handling financial disagreements constructively involves recognizing common sources of conflict, employing effective communication techniques, practicing negotiation and compromise, and seeking professional help when necessary. By addressing these disagreements with empathy, respect, and a commitment to finding mutually acceptable solutions, you can strengthen your relationship and build a more secure and harmonious financial future together.

Now that we've covered financial planning and handling disagreements, let's transition to understanding how external pressures and influences can impact your relationship and ways to navigate them together.

ELEVEN

Addressing External Pressures and Influence

Have you ever felt like your relationship is being pulled in different directions by the expectations and opinions of those around you? External pressures, whether from family, friends, or society at large, can be an invisible yet potent force influencing the dynamics of your relationship. These pressures can shape your decisions, challenge your values, and sometimes even create rifts between you and your partner. Understanding and navigating these external influences is crucial for maintaining a healthy and autonomous relationship.

11.1 Dealing With Family Interference in Relationships

Family can be a source of immense support and love, but they can also, intentionally or not, meddle in your relationship. The first step in dealing with family interference is recognizing the various forms it can take. Unsolicited advice, for example, might come from a place of love and concern but can feel intrusive and undermine your confidence in your decisions. Expectations about how you should live your life, manage your finances, or raise your children can create a sense of obligation and guilt. Overt disapproval or meddling can be more challenging, manifesting as attempts to influence your partner's actions or decisions, creating tension and conflict.

It's essential to differentiate between well-intentioned involvement and problematic interference. Well-intentioned involvement might include occasional advice or support, which can be helpful if it's wanted, respectful, and considerate. Problematic interference, on the other hand, often involves repeated attempts to control or influence your relationship, disregarding your autonomy and boundaries. Recognizing this distinction is crucial for addressing the root causes of interference and maintaining a healthy balance.

Setting boundaries with family members can be challenging, but it is necessary to protect your relationship. Boundaries are not about shutting people out but about creating a respectful space where your relationship can flourish. Start by identifying the specific behaviors or actions that feel intrusive or harmful. Communicate these boundaries clearly and respectfully to your family members. For example, you might say, "We appreciate your concern, but we need to make our own decisions about our finances." It's important to be firm yet empathetic, acknowledging their intentions while asserting your need for independence.

Handling resistance from family members can be difficult, especially if they are used to being heavily involved in your life. It's natural for them to feel hurt or defensive when you set boundaries. Reiterate your appreciation for their support and explain that these boundaries are necessary for your relationship's health. If resistance persists, consider involving a neutral third party, such as a family therapist, to facilitate these conversations and mediate conflicts.

Balancing family expectations with couple autonomy requires navigating cultural or generational differences in views on marriage and relationships. Cultural norms and traditions can deeply influence family expectations, creating pressure to conform to specific roles or behaviors. Generational differences can also play a significant role, with older family members holding onto traditional views that may not align with your values or lifestyle. It's essential to have open and honest conversations with your partner about these expectations and how they impact your relationship.

Work together to develop strategies for managing these differences without compromising your relationship values. For example, if your family expects you to adhere to traditional gender roles, discuss how you can respectfully explain your more egalitarian approach to household responsibilities. Finding common ground and demonstrating how your choices benefit your relationship can help bridge the gap between expectations and autonomy.

Supporting each other against negative family dynamics is crucial for maintaining unity and resilience. When facing criticism or disapproval from family members, presenting a united front can help reinforce your commitment to each other and your decisions. Emotional reassurance is vital in these situations, as feeling unsupported or isolated can exacerbate the stress caused by family interference. Regular check-ins with your partner to discuss how you both feel about family interactions and any ongoing issues can strengthen your bond and provide a safe space to express concerns.

<hr>

Reflection Exercise: Boundary Setting Plan

To navigate family interference effectively, consider creating a Boundary Setting Plan. Take some time with your partner to reflect on the specific areas where you feel family interference is most impactful. Write down the behaviors or actions that feel intrusive or harmful and discuss why these boundaries are important for your relationship. Develop clear and respectful statements to communicate these boundaries to your family members. For instance, if you feel overwhelmed by unsolicited advice, you might say, "We value your input, but we need to make our own decisions about our parenting style."

Finally, discuss how you will handle resistance and support each other in maintaining these boundaries. This plan can serve as a practical guide and a reminder of your commitment to protecting your relationship from external pressures.

11.2 Balancing Individual Friendships and Couple Time

Maintaining individual friendships is not just a healthy addition to your life; it's a necessity. Individual friendships provide a space where you can express parts of yourself that might not always find a place in your romantic relationship. These friendships offer emotional support, a sounding board for your thoughts, and opportunities for personal growth that can enrich your relationship. Imagine having a friend with whom you can share your love for a specific hobby or interest that your partner doesn't quite get. This external support network can also provide a buffer during tough times, giving you additional perspectives and emotional outlets.

Managing time between friends and your partner is where things can get a bit tricky, but it's completely doable with some practical scheduling and open communication. Start by acknowledging that both your relationship and your friendships are important and deserve time and attention. One effective strategy is to create a balanced schedule that allocates specific times for friends and your partner. For instance, you might designate Wednesday nights for dinner with friends and keep Friday evenings for date nights. The key is to communicate these plans openly with your partner, ensuring they understand that your time with friends isn't a threat but a necessary part of a balanced life. Transparency in your schedule helps prevent misunderstandings and reassures your partner of their importance in your life.

Feelings of jealousy or insecurity can occasionally arise when you or your partner spend time with friends. It's natural to feel a twinge of insecurity, especially if the friendship is with someone of the opposite sex or if it seems to take away from your time together. The best approach is to address these feelings openly and honestly. Sit down with your partner and express your feelings without placing blame. For example, you might say, "I sometimes feel a bit left out when you spend a lot of time with your friends. Can we talk about how to balance things better?" This opens up a dialogue where both partners can share their feelings and work towards a solution that reassures both parties. Healthy discussions about these emotions can lead to greater understanding and trust.

Integrating social circles can be a wonderful way to bridge the gap between individual friendships and couple time. When appropriate, consider inviting your friends to join you and your partner in activities. This can help create a more inclusive social network where everyone feels connected and valued. For example, hosting a game night, going on group outings, or even planning a weekend getaway with friends and your partner can foster a sense of community. These shared experiences can reduce feelings of separation or exclusion and allow your partner to build their own relationships with your friends. It can also help friends see your partner as an integral part of your life, fostering mutual respect and understanding.

Interactive Element: Friendship and Relationship Balance Journal

To help navigate the balance between individual friendships and couple time, consider keeping a Friendship and Relationship Balance Journal. Start by logging your weekly activities, noting the time spent with friends and your partner. Reflect on how these interactions make you feel and whether you think the balance is healthy. Are there weeks where you feel more connected to your friends but distant from your partner, or vice versa? Use these reflections to adjust your schedule and find a balance that feels right for both of you. Sharing your journal entries with your partner can also open up discussions about how to support each other in maintaining these important relationships.

Balancing individual friendships and couple time requires ongoing effort and communication, but it's a crucial aspect of a healthy relationship. By valuing your friendships, managing your time wisely, addressing insecurities openly, and integrating social circles, you can create a harmonious balance that supports both your personal growth and your partnership.

11.3 Confronting Societal Expectations as a Couple

Navigating the sea of societal expectations can feel overwhelming for many couples. Society often imposes a set of predefined milestones and markers of success, such as getting married by a certain age, having children, achieving career milestones, and adhering to specific lifestyle choices. These pressures can be subtle, like the well-meaning questions from friends and family about when you plan to have kids, or more overt, like the pervasive cultural narratives that equate career success with personal worth. The impact of these pressures can be profound, affecting both individual well-being and the dynamics of your relationship. They can create stress, guilt, and a sense of failure if you feel you're not meeting these external standards, leading to conflicts and dissatisfaction within the relationship.

One of the most empowering steps you can take as a couple is to critically evaluate these societal norms and make decisions based on your own values and priorities. This means taking a step back and asking yourselves what truly matters to you as individuals and as a couple, rather than simply conforming to what is expected. For some, this might mean choosing a non-traditional path, such as deciding not to have children or opting for a lifestyle that prioritizes experiences over material possessions. For others, it might involve redefining roles within the relationship, such as sharing responsibilities in a way that defies traditional gender norms. The key is to have open, honest conversations about your desires and aspirations and to support each other in making choices that align with your authentic selves.

Building resilience against criticism and judgment from others is essential for maintaining your course. It's natural to encounter resistance or disapproval when you deviate from societal norms, but internal validation and mutual support are powerful tools for staying grounded. Start by cultivating a strong sense of self-worth and confidence in your decisions. This involves regularly affirming the validity and importance of your choices and reminding each other why these decisions are right for you. When faced with criticism, try to view it as a reflection of the other person's perspectives and biases rather than a judgment of your worth or the viability of your choices.

Developing a resilient mindset can be further supported by surrounding yourselves with a community of like-minded individuals who share similar values and can provide encouragement and affirmation. This community doesn't have to be large; it can be a few close friends or a support group where you feel understood and accepted. Engaging with others who have faced and navigated similar societal pressures can offer valuable insights and reassurance that you're not alone in your journey.

Advocating for your relationship choices in social settings can sometimes feel daunting, especially when faced with intrusive questions or unsolicited advice. However, equipping yourselves with tools to handle these situations can make a significant difference. Start by preparing responses to common questions or comments that respect both your choices and the other person's curiosity. For instance, when asked about your plans to have children—a deeply personal question—you can choose how direct you want to be. A softer approach might be, "We've decided to focus on our careers and personal growth for now." However, if you'd prefer a more direct response, you might simply say, "We aren't." Both options allow you to assert your choices with confidence, depending on your comfort level, while keeping the conversation respectful and without being confrontational.

Educating others about your perspectives can also be empowering. This doesn't mean you have to justify your decisions to everyone, but sharing your reasoning with those who are genuinely interested can promote understanding and respect. For instance, if you've chosen a non-traditional career path, explaining how it aligns with your values and goals can help others see the thoughtfulness behind your decision. Approach these conversations with openness and a willingness to listen, creating a dialogue rather than a debate. This not only helps others understand your choices but also reinforces your commitment to living authentically.

In summary, confronting societal expectations requires a combination of self-reflection, mutual support, and resilience. By identifying the pressures you face, making personal choices that align with your values, building resilience against criticism, and advocating for your relationship choices, you can navigate these external influences with confidence and integrity. This chapter has explored the various ways in which external pressures can impact your relationship and provided strategies for maintaining your autonomy and well-being. In the next chapter, we will delve into the importance of healing and growth post-conflict, offering tools to turn challenges into opportunities for deeper connection and understanding.

TWELVE

Healing and Growth Post-Conflict

H ave you ever found yourself stuck in the aftermath of a conflict, unsure how to move forward? It's a feeling many of us know all too well. Conflicts, though inevitable, often leave lingering wounds that can fester if not addressed properly. This chapter delves into the transformative power of forgiveness, a key component in healing and growing from these conflicts. Forgiveness is more than just a word; it's a process that can help release resentment and pave the way for a more peaceful, connected relationship.

12.1 The Healing Power of Forgiveness

UNDERSTANDING FORGIVENESS IN RELATIONSHIPS: Conflict can leave emotional scars that, if left untreated, can turn into long-term damage. Forgiveness plays a crucial role in mitigating this damage. It acts as a balm, soothing the hurt and allowing both parties to move forward. But it's essential to distinguish between forgiving and forgetting. Forgiving is about letting go of the resentment and anger that hold you back, while forgetting, which implies erasing the memory of the hurt, isn't always possible or even advisable. Genuine forgiveness involves remembering the event but choosing to release its hold on your emotions. It's a conscious decision to encourage peace and emotional freedom.

. . .

STEPS TO EFFECTIVE FORGIVING: Forgiveness is a journey that begins with acknowledgment. Start by recognizing the hurt and its impact on you. This isn't about wallowing in pain but about understanding its roots. Next, practice empathy. Try to see the situation from your partner's perspective, which can help humanize them and reduce feelings of anger. Once you've reached this point, make the decision to forgive. This doesn't mean condoning the hurtful behavior but choosing to let go of the negative emotions attached to it. One effective exercise is to write a letter to your partner, expressing your feelings and your decision to forgive. You don't have to give them the letter; the act of writing can be cathartic and help solidify your commitment to moving forward.

FORGIVENESS AND EMOTIONAL HEALTH: The act of forgiving has profound benefits for your emotional health. Studies have shown that forgiveness can reduce stress, lower blood pressure, and even improve immune function. By letting go of grudges, you free up emotional energy that can be redirected toward positive interactions and personal growth. Forgiveness fosters an environment where happiness and emotional well-being can flourish. Renowned psychologist Dr. Everett Worthington, who has extensively researched the topic, emphasizes that forgiveness can lead to increased life satisfaction and lower levels of depression and anxiety. The therapeutic benefits of forgiveness are well-documented and provide a compelling case for its practice in maintaining a healthy relationship.

CHALLENGES TO FORGIVING: Forgiveness is not always easy. Deep-seated anger, feelings of betrayal, and repeated offenses can make the process incredibly challenging. It's important to recognize these obstacles and address them head-on. Deep-seated anger often stems from unresolved issues or past traumas. In such cases, professional help from a therapist can be invaluable in unpacking these feelings and finding a path to forgiveness. Betrayal can shatter the foundation of trust in a relationship, making forgiveness seem impossible. Here, it's crucial to rebuild trust step-by-step, ensuring that both partners are committed to the process. Repeated offenses can erode the willingness to forgive. Setting clear boundaries and consequences for repeated behaviors can address this challenge. Forgiveness is a personal journey, and it's essential to move at your own pace, acknowledging that it's okay to seek help when needed.

Forgiveness Reflection Exercise

Objective: To facilitate the process of forgiveness and emotional healing.

1. **ACKNOWLEDGE THE HURT:** Write down what happened, how it made you feel, and its impact on your relationship.
2. **EMPATHIZE:** Reflect on your partner's perspective. What might have driven their actions? This isn't about justifying their behavior but understanding it.
3. **DECIDE TO FORGIVE:** Write a letter to your partner expressing your feelings and your decision to forgive. You can choose whether to share it with them or keep it as a personal commitment.
4. **RELEASE:** Engage in a symbolic act of letting go, such as tearing up the letter or burning it (safely), to signify releasing the negative emotions associated with the hurt.
5. **REFLECT:** Spend some quiet time reflecting on how you feel after the exercise. Note any changes in your emotional state and feelings towards your partner.

Forgiveness is a powerful tool for healing and growth in any relationship. By understanding its role, following a structured approach, and recognizing the benefits it brings to emotional health, you can navigate the complexities of conflict with grace and compassion.

12.2 Learning From Past Conflicts for Future Harmony

Have you ever noticed that some arguments seem to replay like a broken record? If so, you're not alone. Conflicts often stem from recurring patterns and triggers that, once identified, can be managed more effectively. To analyze these patterns, start by reflecting on past disputes. Note the circumstances, emotions, and outcomes of each conflict. Were they often sparked by similar issues, such as money, chores, or time management? Create a conflict map by writing down each argument and identifying common themes or triggers. This visual representation can help you see the bigger picture and understand the underlying issues that fuel these disputes.

Once you've mapped out your conflicts, it's crucial to dive deeper into understanding the root causes. Often, surface-level disagreements are symptoms of deeper, unresolved issues. For instance, arguments about household chores might actually be about feeling undervalued or unsupported. By identifying these core issues, you can address the real problems rather than just the symptoms. Discuss with your partner what each conflict means to you. Are there unmet needs or unspoken fears driving your reactions? Open, honest conversations about these deeper issues can pave the way for more meaningful resolutions.

With a clearer understanding of your conflict patterns, the next step is to develop tailored conflict resolution strategies. Start by focusing on proactive communication skills. This means discussing potential issues before they escalate into full-blown arguments. Regular check-ins can help you stay in tune with each other's feelings and concerns. When disagreements do arise, practice emotional regulation techniques like deep breathing or taking a short break to cool down. This helps prevent the escalation of tension and keeps the discussion productive. Compromise is another vital skill. It's important to find a middle ground where both partners feel heard and respected. This might mean taking turns managing tasks or agreeing on a budget that respects both partners' financial habits.

Creating a personalized conflict resolution plan can be incredibly helpful. Begin by outlining steps to take when a conflict arises. This might include agreeing to take a five-minute pause if the argument becomes too heated or committing to using "I" statements to express feelings without blame. Detail how to de-escalate tension—this could involve physical touch like holding hands, which can be a simple yet powerful way to reconnect emotionally. The plan should also include strategies for engaging in productive dialogue. Establish ground rules, such as no interrupting and no name-calling. Setting these rules in advance helps create a safe space for open discussion, making it easier to resolve issues constructively.

Conflict resolution is not a one-time fix but an ongoing process. Regularly reviewing and adjusting your strategies is crucial as your relationship evolves. What worked in the early stages of your relationship might not be as effective later on. Schedule periodic reviews of your conflict resolution plan. Discuss what's working and what isn't, and be open to making changes. Continually learning and adapting helps you stay responsive to each other's needs and behaviors. This ongoing commitment to improvement cultivates a relationship environment where both partners feel valued and understood.

Conflict Analysis Exercise

Objective: To identify patterns and triggers in past conflicts for better understanding and resolution.

1. **MAP OUT CONFLICTS:** Write down each significant argument you've had. Note the date, the issue, and the outcome.
2. **IDENTIFY PATTERNS:** Look for recurring themes or triggers. Are there specific topics that frequently lead to disputes?
3. **DISCUSS UNDERLYING ISSUES:** Talk with your partner about what these conflicts mean to you. Are there deeper, unresolved issues driving these arguments?
4. **DEVELOP STRATEGIES:** Based on your analysis, create tailored conflict resolution strategies. Focus on proactive communication, emotional regulation, and compromise.
5. **REVIEW AND ADJUST:** Regularly review your conflict resolution plan. Discuss what's working, what isn't, and make necessary adjustments.

By taking the time to analyze past conflicts, develop tailored strategies, and continually adapt, you can turn disputes into opportunities for growth and harmony in your relationship.

12.3 When to Seek Professional Help

There are times when the complexity of relationship issues surpasses what you and your partner can handle alone. But how do you know when it's time to bring in a professional? One key sign is recurring conflicts that never seem to find resolution, no matter how many times you address them. It's like being stuck in a loop where the same arguments keep resurfacing, leaving you both feeling frustrated and helpless. Another red flag is an inability to move past old hurts. If you find that past grievances keep cropping up in new arguments, it might indicate that those wounds haven't fully healed. Additionally, if conflicts are impacting your mental health—causing anxiety, depression, or excessive stress—it's a clear signal that professional help might be needed.

The world of professional support offers various avenues, each tailored to different needs and circumstances. Couples therapy is one of the most common forms of support. In couples therapy, a licensed therapist works with both partners to address relationship issues, improve communication, and develop healthier interaction patterns. Therapy sessions typically involve both partners, but individual sessions might also be recommended. Mediation is another option, especially useful for couples dealing with specific issues like financial disputes or co-parenting challenges. A mediator helps both parties come to a mutual agreement without taking sides. Relationship coaching, on the other hand, focuses more on setting and achieving relationship goals. Coaches provide strategies and tools for improving relationship dynamics, much like a life coach but with a focus on romantic partnerships. Choosing the right type of professional support depends on your specific situation and what you hope to achieve. If you're unsure, consulting with a professional for an initial assessment can provide clarity on the best path forward.

Preparing for therapy or counseling is an important step to ensure you get the most out of it. Start by setting clear goals. What do you hope to achieve? Whether it's improving communication, resolving a specific issue, or rebuilding trust, having clear objectives will guide your sessions. Being open to change is crucial. Therapy often involves looking at things from a new perspective, which can be challenging but necessary for growth. Honesty is another cornerstone. Be prepared to share your thoughts and feelings openly. This might feel uncomfortable at first, but transparency is vital for effective therapy. Before your first session, discuss with your partner what you both want to share and what you hope to gain. This pre-therapy conversation can set a positive tone and align your expectations.

Integrating professional advice into your relationship dynamics requires commitment and consistency. After each therapy session, discuss the insights and strategies you've learned with your partner. How can you apply them to your daily interactions? For example, if your therapist suggests active listening techniques, consciously practice these during your conversations. It's about making small, consistent changes that gradually transform your relationship. Monitoring progress is equally important. Set aside time to reflect on what's working and what's not. Regular check-ins can help you stay on track and make necessary adjustments. It's also beneficial to revisit your therapist periodically, even after you've made significant progress. This helps reinforce the changes and address any new issues that might arise. Remember, the goal is not just to resolve current conflicts but to develop a toolkit of strategies that will help you navigate future challenges more effectively.

Seeking professional help is not a sign of failure but a proactive step towards strengthening your relationship. It shows a commitment to growth and a willingness to invest in your future together. By recognizing the signs that you might need help, understanding the types of support available, preparing for therapy, and integrating professional advice into your daily life, you can turn challenges into opportunities for deeper connection and mutual growth.

12.4 Renewing Commitment After Turmoil

REAFFIRMING COMMITMENT: After a conflict, reaffirming your commitment to each other can be a powerful act of unity and healing. This doesn't have to be a grand gesture; it can be as simple as sitting down together and openly discussing your commitment to the relationship. Start by sharing what you value most about each other and your partnership. Consider setting new relationship goals that reflect your shared vision for the future. Whether it's planning more quality time together or working on a joint project, these goals can provide a renewed sense of purpose and direction. Some couples find it meaningful to renew their vows, either privately or with loved ones, as a way to reinforce their dedication. Another idea is to create a vision board together, filled with images and words that represent your hopes and dreams for your relationship. This visual reminder can serve as a constant source of inspiration and motivation.

CELEBRATING THE RENEWED COMMITMENT: Once you've reaffirmed your commitment, it's important to celebrate this milestone in a way that feels significant to both of you. This could be as elaborate as planning a trip to a place that holds special meaning or as simple as creating a new ritual that symbolizes your renewed dedication. Some couples might enjoy a weekend getaway to reconnect and create new memories. Others might prefer a quiet evening at home, cooking a favorite meal and reminiscing about the positive moments in their relationship. The key is to choose a celebration that feels authentic and meaningful. You might also consider incorporating a small ceremony, even if it's just the two of you, where you exchange heartfelt words or tokens that symbolize your commitment. These rituals, no matter how big or small, can serve as powerful reminders of the strength and resilience of your bond.

ONGOING COMMITMENT PRACTICES: Maintaining a strong commitment requires ongoing effort and intentionality. One effective practice is regular relationship check-ins. These can be weekly or monthly conversations where you both share how you're feeling about the relationship, discuss any concerns, and celebrate your successes. These check-ins can help prevent small issues from escalating and keep you both aligned on your goals. Continuing to date each other is another crucial practice. Whether it's a weekly date night or spontaneous acts of love, making time for each other helps keep the romance alive. Always working on communication skills, such as active listening and expressing gratitude, can also strengthen your bond. Consider attending workshops or reading books together on relationship skills to keep learning and growing. These ongoing practices ensure that your commitment remains strong and vibrant, even in the face of challenges.

SUPPORT SYSTEMS AND COMMUNITY INVOLVEMENT: In addition to your personal efforts, involving support systems and community resources can further reinforce your commitment. Engaging with support groups, whether in-person or online, can provide valuable encouragement and guidance. These groups offer a space to share experiences, learn from others, and gain new perspectives. Community involvement, such as participating in couple's workshops or retreats, can also be beneficial. These events provide structured opportunities to deepen your connection and learn new skills. Additionally, having a network of friends and family who support your relationship can be invaluable. They can offer a listening ear, practical advice, and a sense of belonging. Building and maintaining these external support systems can provide a safety net of encouragement and resilience, reinforcing your commitment and helping you navigate any challenges that arise.

Renewing your commitment after a conflict is a powerful way to reinforce your bond and set a positive path forward. By reaffirming your dedication, celebrating your renewed commitment, maintaining ongoing practices, and involving supportive systems, you can strengthen your relationship and create a resilient, loving partnership. As we move to the next chapter, we'll explore strategies for maintaining relationship satisfaction over time, ensuring that your bond continues to grow and flourish.

THIRTEEN

Maintaining Relationship Satisfaction Over Time

H ave you ever wondered how many times, throughout this book, I've asked you, "Have you ever wondered...''? Well, this time, it's different. As we reach the final chapter, let's dive deeper: Have you ever wondered what it takes for a relationship to not just survive, but thrive through the challenges and joys of life together? The secret often lies in the regular maintenance of the relationship, much like how you would care for a cherished garden. One of the most effective ways to ensure your relationship remains vibrant and fulfilling is through annual relationship check-ins. These check-ins act as a structured time to reflect on the past year, celebrate successes, and set new goals, providing a roadmap for continued growth and satisfaction.

13.1 Annual Relationship Check-ins and Goals

Regular check-ins are crucial for assessing satisfaction levels, addressing emerging issues, and reinforcing your partnership's strengths. Think of it as a yearly health check-up for your relationship. During these check-ins, you can openly discuss what has been working well and what areas might need some attention. This proactive approach helps prevent small issues from snowballing into major conflicts and ensures that both partners feel heard and valued.

To conduct effective check-ins, set a comfortable, distraction-free environment where you can both relax and focus on each other. This could be a cozy corner of your home, a favorite café, or even a serene outdoor spot. Use open-ended questions to explore each partner's feelings and experiences over the past year. Questions like "What moments made you feel most connected to me?", "Are there any unmet needs or concerns you have?" and "How can we support each other better?" can open up meaningful dialogues. Avoid rushing through this process; take your time to listen and reflect.

Setting relationship goals during these check-ins can be a powerful way to keep your relationship dynamic and evolving. These goals should be actionable and meaningful, addressing both individual and shared aspirations. For instance, you might set a goal to improve communication by practicing active listening techniques or to spend more quality time together by planning regular date nights. Additionally, working on individual areas of growth, such as pursuing a new hobby or taking a course, can positively impact the relationship by fostering personal fulfillment and self-confidence.

Documenting your progress and the outcomes of these check-ins can serve as a motivating record of growth and a way to celebrate your successes together. Keeping a relationship journal or creating a digital document where you note key points from each check-in can be incredibly beneficial. This record helps you track your journey and provides a tangible reminder of your commitment to each other. Reviewing these notes can be particularly uplifting during challenging times, reminding you of the progress you've made and the goals you've achieved.

Recognizing signs of progress is essential for maintaining momentum and motivation. Look for concrete improvements in areas like communication, emotional intimacy, dispute resolution, and mutual support. For example, you might notice that disagreements are resolved more quickly or that you feel more emotionally connected during daily interactions. Acknowledge these positive changes during your check-ins and celebrate them as a couple. Reflecting on these signals can reinforce your efforts and encourage continued growth.

Visual Element: Relationship Check-In Template

Annual Relationship Check-In Template

ENVIRONMENT:

- Choose a distraction-free setting (e.g., cozy corner, favorite café).

OPEN-ENDED QUESTIONS:

- "What moments made you feel most connected to me?"
- "Are there any unmet needs or concerns you have?"
- "How can we support each other better?"

SETTING GOALS:

- Relationship Goals: (e.g., improve communication, plan regular date nights)
- Individual Goals: (e.g., pursue a new hobby, take a course)

DOCUMENTING PROGRESS:

- Relationship Journal/Digital Document
- Key Points From Each Check-In
- Review Notes During Challenging Times

- Improvements in Communication
- Enhanced Emotional Intimacy
- Efficient Dispute Resolution
- Increased Mutual Support

Regular check-ins, effective goal-setting, and celebrating progress can help you maintain relationship satisfaction over time, ensuring that your partnership remains resilient and fulfilling.

13.2 Keeping the Spark Alive in Everyday Life

Have you ever noticed how the smallest gestures can have the most significant impact? Daily gestures of love are like tiny stitches that hold the fabric of your relationship together. Imagine the warmth you feel when you find a love note tucked into your lunch bag or receive a thoughtful text out of the blue. These small acts convey love and appreciation, showing your partner that you're thinking of them even amidst the chaos of daily life. Preparing their favorite meal or simply making them a cup of coffee in the morning can speak volumes. These gestures don't require grand efforts but have a cumulative effect, reinforcing the emotional bond day by day.

Incorporating surprise and variety into your relationship can keep things exciting and prevent the monotony that often settles in over time.

Maintaining Relationship Satisfaction Over Time • 105

Picture this: planning an unexpected outing to a place your partner has always wanted to visit or surprising them with a gift that shows you've been paying attention to their interests. Spontaneous acts of kindness, like planning a weekend getaway or organizing a surprise date night, can reignite the spark and add a sense of adventure to your relationship. Variety doesn't always mean extravagant; even small changes, like trying a new restaurant or exploring a different part of town, can bring a fresh perspective and renewed excitement.

Regular date nights are crucial for maintaining one-on-one time, no matter how busy life gets. It's easy to let the demands of work, family, and other responsibilities overshadow your relationship. Carving out time for regular dates ensures that you and your partner can reconnect and focus solely on each other. The key is consistency and making these moments a priority amidst your hectic schedules.

Sustaining physical and emotional intimacy over the long term requires ongoing effort and communication. Physical touch is a powerful way to maintain connection, whether it's through holding hands, hugging, or cuddling. These small acts of physical affection can foster a sense of security and closeness. Equally important is maintaining open communication about each partner's evolving needs and desires. As time passes, these needs may change, and it's essential to discuss them openly without judgment. Regularly checking in with each other about what feels good, what might need adjustment, and how you can support each other's intimacy can keep the connection strong.

The power of small gestures, the thrill of surprises, the consistency of date nights, and the nurturing of physical and emotional intimacy all play vital roles in keeping the spark alive in your relationship. These practices remind you and your partner of the love you share and the commitment you've made to each other. They create a continuous cycle of giving and receiving love, reinforcing the bond that holds you together through the everyday challenges and joys of life.

13.4 Embracing Changes and Growing Together

Life is full of changes, and whether it's children growing up, job changes, or moving to a new city, these transitions can significantly impact your relationship. Anticipating these changes and discussing them openly can help you adapt together. For instance, if you're considering a job change that requires relocation, talk about how this move will affect your daily routines, social circles, and overall lifestyle. Planning together for these shifts ensures that both partners feel involved and prepared rather than blindsided or overwhelmed. It's about being proactive and considering each other's needs and concerns.

Adopting a growth mindset in your relationship means being open to learning and evolving together. This mindset encourages you to view challenges as opportunities for growth rather than obstacles. When you approach your relationship with this attitude, you're more likely to embrace change positively. For example, if one of you decides to go back to school, instead of seeing it solely as a disruption, you can view it as an opportunity for personal development that will enrich both of your lives. This mindset fosters resilience and adaptability, making you stronger as a couple.

Supporting each other's personal and professional growth is crucial for a healthy relationship. When one partner decides to pursue a new career path or take up a new hobby, the other partner's support can make all the difference. This support can be as simple as offering words of encouragement, helping to free up time by sharing more household responsibilities or attending events related to your partner's interests. This mutual support boosts individual growth and strengthens the relationship by showing that you're invested in each other's happiness and success.

Navigating difficult times together can be challenging, but it also offers a chance to deepen your connection. During tough periods, such as dealing with a family illness or financial stress, staying connected and supportive is essential. Communicate openly about your fears, hopes, and needs. Lean on each other for emotional support and practical help. For instance, if one of you loses a job, discuss how you can adjust your budget together and explore new job opportunities. Use these experiences to build trust and demonstrate your commitment to each other, turning adversity into a bonding experience rather than a source of division.

13.5 Celebrating Milestones and Creating New Traditions

Recognizing and celebrating key milestones in your relationship is more than just marking time; it's about acknowledging your journey together and reinforcing your bond. Think about the joy of celebrating an anniversary, remembering the day you first met, or marking significant achievements like buying your first home or welcoming a child. These celebrations serve as important reminders of the love and commitment you share. They provide an opportunity to reflect on the growth you've experienced together and to express gratitude for each other's presence in your lives. Whether it's a romantic dinner, a weekend getaway, or simply a heartfelt conversation, these moments of recognition can reignite the spark and bring a renewed sense of appreciation.

Creating meaningful traditions can add a layer of depth and continuity to your relationship. These traditions don't have to be grand or elaborate; they just need to be meaningful to both of you. Perhaps you start a tradition of taking an annual vacation to a place you both love, or you establish a special holiday ritual that becomes something you look forward to every year. Weekly routines, like a Sunday morning walk or a Friday night movie, can also create a rhythm of connection that helps you stay grounded amidst the busyness of life. These traditions become shared experiences that you both can rely on, providing a sense of stability and continuity that strengthens your bond.

Involving family and friends in your celebrations can enrich these experiences and build a supportive community around your relationship. Imagine the joy of having your closest friends and family members join you in celebrating your anniversary or a significant achievement. This inclusion amplifies the celebration and brings a sense of shared joy and support. Hosting a small gathering or a dinner party can be a wonderful way to celebrate together, creating memories that include the people who matter most to you. This communal aspect of celebration reinforces the idea that your relationship is part of a larger network of love and support.

Documenting and reflecting on your milestones can serve as cherished memories and reminders of your journey and growth. Keeping a scrapbook, a photo album, or even a digital collection of memories can provide a tangible record of your shared experiences. This documentation allows you to look back on the moments that have defined your relationship, from the small, everyday joys to the significant milestones. Reflecting on these memories together can be a powerful way to reconnect and remember why you fell in love in the first place. It also provides a source of inspiration and motivation during challenging times, reminding you of the strength and resilience of your bond.

As you celebrate milestones and create new traditions, you build a rich tapestry of shared experiences that reinforce your connection and deepen your bond. These practices honor your past and present and lay a strong foundation for the future, ensuring that your relationship continues to thrive and grow. By recognizing and celebrating your journey together, you affirm your commitment and create a legacy of love and joy that will sustain you through all of life's ups and downs.

Conclusion

As we bring this journey to a close, let's reflect on the path we've traveled together. From the early chapters on effective communication to the deeper dives into trust, conflict resolution, financial planning, and maintaining relationship satisfaction, each chapter has been a stepping stone toward building a stronger, more fulfilling partnership.

We began by exploring the foundations of effective communication. Understanding how to truly listen and express oneself without causing conflict can transform the way you and your partner connect. Through active listening, expressing needs constructively, and being mindful of nonverbal cues, you've learned how to create a dialogue that's both open and respectful.

Next, we delved into the importance of trust. Trust is the bedrock of any relationship, and building it requires consistency, reliability, honesty, and integrity. We've discussed how to maintain trust through life's challenges and how to rebuild it when it has been fractured. The exercises and strategies provided will help you fortify this essential element in your relationship.

Conflict is inevitable, but how you handle it can make all the difference. By identifying root causes, employing healthy argumentation techniques, and using timeout protocols, you've been equipped with tools to turn conflicts into opportunities for growth. Remember, it's not about avoiding disagreements but navigating them in a way that strengthens your bond.

Financial planning can be a delicate topic, but it's crucial for long-term stability. Through joint budgeting, setting financial goals, and handling disagreements constructively, you've learned how to approach money matters as a team. The goal is to create a financial foundation that supports both your individual aspirations and your shared dreams.

Maintaining relationship satisfaction over time requires ongoing effort and intentionality. Annual relationship check-ins, keeping the spark alive through daily gestures, and cultivating mutual hobbies and interests are just a few ways to ensure that your relationship continues to thrive. Embracing changes and celebrating milestones together can help you grow as a couple, creating a rich tapestry of shared experiences.

Key takeaways from this book include the importance of open, honest communication, the role of trust and how to build it, effective conflict resolution strategies, collaborative financial planning, and continuous efforts to keep your relationship vibrant and satisfying. Each chapter has offered practical exercises and strategies to help you apply these concepts in your daily life.

But the journey doesn't end here. Continuous learning and application are essential. Keep the conversation going with your partner, regularly revisit the strategies you've learned, and don't hesitate to seek external support when needed. Therapists, financial advisors, and even trusted friends can provide valuable insights and guidance.

Personal growth is just as important as the work you do together. Investing in your own self-care and development ensures that you have the emotional and mental bandwidth to nurture your relationship. Take time to pursue your passions, reflect on your personal goals, and practice self-compassion. A healthy, fulfilled individual is better equipped to contribute to a healthy, fulfilling relationship.

As a call to action, I encourage you to start implementing at least one strategy or exercise from each chapter immediately. Whether it's practicing active listening, setting up a joint budget, or planning a surprise date night, taking action is the first step toward positive change. Small, consistent efforts can lead to significant improvements over time.

Your experiences and successes are valuable, not just to you but to others who may be on a similar journey. I invite you to share your stories, insights, and feedback. By creating a sense of community and shared learning, we can all benefit from each other's experiences. Your journey can inspire others and create a ripple effect of positive change.

Finally, I want to express my heartfelt gratitude. Thank you for embarking on this journey to strengthen your relationship. Your commitment to improving your partnership is commendable, and I hope the tools and insights provided in this book serve you well. Remember, every step you take towards a healthier relationship is a step towards a more fulfilling and joyful life together.

From my own experiences amidst the natural beauty of Switzerland to the lessons learned through life's challenges, I've seen firsthand the transformative power of trust, connection, and continuous growth. Life teaches us that every crisis is an opportunity, and maintaining a relaxed and aware mind is key to growth. I hope you find these principles as useful in your journey as they have been in mine.

Here's to your continued growth, love, and happiness. Keep nurturing your relationship, investing in yourselves, and celebrating the beautiful journey you're on together. Thank you for allowing me to be a part of it.

Keeping the Connection Alive

Now that you have everything you need to overcome emotional distance, rebuild trust, and improve communication in your relationship, it's time to share your newfound knowledge and guide other couples to the same help.

If you've already left a review for *From Conflict to Closeness—The Couples Therapy Playbook*, thank you! If not, well... shame on you! Just kidding! But seriously, reviews help other couples find the guidance they need, just like you did. Simply by leaving your honest opinion on Amazon, you'll be showing other couples where they can find the support they're looking for and passing on your passion for building stronger, more fulfilling relationships.

Thank you for being so helpful. Sharing what we've learned keeps the bond between couples alive, and you're helping us to do just that.

References

Puhlman, B. (2017). The role of emotional intelligence in signed language interpreting. https://core.ac.uk/download/228830864.pdf

Emotional Intelligence - Navigating College Relationships - GradesAI: Boost Your Grades, Make Studying Effortless, Regardless of Your Learning Level.. https://gradesai.com/emotional-intelligence-navigating-college-relationships/

Knight, W. (2018). Building Empathy. Apress EBooks. https://doi.org/10.1007/978-1-4842-4227-8_7

Release Your Painful Secrets and Improve Your Relationships - Mag Love. https://mag-love.com/relationship-advice/release-your-painful-secrets-and-improve-your-relationships/

10 Unconventional Yet Effective Health Remedies You Should Try Today. https://healthremediesforall.com/article/10-unconventional-yet-effective-health-remedies-you-should-try-today

Transforming Retail: Building a Stakeholder Strategy for Sustainable Success. https://mindfulretail.ca/blog/transforming-retail--building-a-stakeholder-strategy-for-sustainable-success

Mental Health Support for Healthcare Professionals | GetMed Staffing. https://www.getmedstaffing.com/blog/mental-health-support-healthcare-professionals

Setting up Service Level Agreements - Pia-K Strategi och Design. https://pia-k.se/setting-up-service-level-agreements/

Jayakrishnan, R., Gopal, G. N., & Santhikrishna, M. S. (2018). Multi-Class Emotion Detection and Annotation in Malayalam Novels. https://doi.org/10.1109/iccci.2018.8441492

Practical Tips to Overcome Self-Esteem Issues in Marriage. https://mantracare.org/therapy/relationship/self-esteem-issues-in-marriage/

The Power of Forgiveness: Why It's Essential During the Holidays by Michelle Donice Gillis, Ph. D.. https://www.thenorthstarllc.com/post/the-power-of-forgiveness-why-it-s-essential-during-the-holidays

5 Questions to Address in Marriage Counseling: Expert Advice. https://cardinalpointcounseling.com/5-questions-marriage-counseling/

Episode 280 - How To Keep The Romance Alive in Marriage - Amanda Louder Coaching. https://amandalouder.com/podcast/280/

The Importance of Communication and Listening in a Happy Marriage - Marry on chain. https://marryonchain.com/p/articles/the-importance-of-communication-and-listening-in-a-happy-marriage

Achieving Relationship Goals: Tips for Creating a Fulfilling Relationship. https://www.greetsapp.com/blog/achieving-relationship-goals-tips-for-creating-a-fulfilling-relationship

The Power of Journaling for Stress Relief. https://careclinic.io/journaling-for-stress-relief/

How to Find My Hobby? – A.Z.A.Y. https://www.azay.com.au/how-to-find-my-hobby/

How to Be Emotionally Intelligent in Love Relationships https://www.helpguide.org/articles/mental-health/emotional-intelligence-love-relationships.htm

Attachment Styles and How They Affect Adult Relationships https://www.helpguide.org/articles/relationships-communication/attachment-and-adult-relationships.htm

Nonviolent communication: The scientifically proven, step-by https://qz.com/838321/nonviolent-communication-the-scientifically-proven-step-by-step-guide-to-having-a-breakthrough-conversation-across-party-lines

33 Couples Therapy Exercises, Activities & Questions https://www.carepatron.com/guides/couples-therapy-exercises

Healthy Communication Tips - Relationships https://www.verywellmind.com/managing-conflict-in-relationships-communication-tips-3144967

17 Communication Exercises for Couples Therapy https://www.talkspace.com/blog/communication-exercises-for-couples-therapy/

The Power Of Gestures: Non-Verbal Communication In https://www.

betterhelp.com/advice/relations/the-power-of-gestures-non-verbal-communication-in-relationships/

Conflict Resolution in Relationships & Couples: 5 Strategies https://positivepsychology.com/conflict-resolution-relationships/

How To Communicate In A Relationship https://www.forbes.com/health/wellness/how-to-communicate-in-a-relationship/

What Are Triggers, and How Do They Form? - Psych Central https://psychcentral.com/lib/what-is-a-trigger

Resolving Conflict in Marriage--A Case Study - Roger K Allen* https://www.rogerkallen.com/resolving-conflict-in-marriage-a-case-study/

Using Mindfulness and Self-Reflection in Couples Counselling https://couplescounsellingcentre.com/individual-therapy/using-mindfulness-and-self-reflection-in-couples-counselling/

How communication can build and improve relationships? https://29k.org/article/effective-communication-strategies-for-building-and-improving-relationships

Betrayal Trauma: Signs and How to Start Healing - Healthline https://www.healthline.com/health/mental-health/betrayal-trauma

Why Vulnerability in Relationships Is So Important https://www.verywellmind.com/why-vulnerability-in-relationships-is-so-important-5193728

Should You Have an Accountability Partner? https://www.wgu.edu/blog/should-you-have-accountability-partner2305.html

Daily Rituals of Connection - The Gottman Institute https://www.gottman.com/blog/3-daily-rituals-that-stop-spouses-from-taking-each-other-for-granted/

5 Effective Communication Techniques for Couples https://www.counsellinginmelbourne.com.au/communication-techniques-for-couples/

Synchronized affect in shared experiences strengthens https://www.nature.com/articles/s42003-023-05461-2

Enhancing Sexual Intimacy in Long-Term Relationships https://www.marriagefamilyservices.com/post/enhancing-sexual-intimacy-in-long-term-relationships/

The Importance of Self-Care in a Healthy Relationship https://www.couplescounselingchicago.net/self-care-healthy-relationship/

How to Overcome Insecurities: 10 Tips to Improve Your https://www.betterup.com/blog/how-to-overcome-insecurities

Setting Healthy Boundaries in Relationships https://www.helpguide.org/articles/relationships-communication/setting-healthy-boundaries-in-relationships.htm

Individual Therapy To Improve All Of Your Relationships https://
greenpointpsychotherapy.com/individual-therapy-to-improve-all-of-your-
relationships/

Effective Strategies for Financial Communication: A Guide https://
berkshiremm.com/effective-strategies-for-financial-communication-a-
guide-to-financial-conversations-for-couples/

3 Budget Apps for Couples Who Want to Sync on Money https://
www.nerdwallet.com/article/finance/3-budget-apps-for-couples-who-
want-to-align-on-money

How to Resolve Financial Stress in Your Relationship https://www.
healthyminds.nyc/blog/how-to-resolve-financial-stress-in-your-relationship

Love & Money: 5 steps to help couples strengthen financial https://
www.360financialliteracy.org/Topics/Spending-Saving/Goal-Setting/
Love-Money-5-steps-to-help-couples-

Made in the USA
Coppell, TX
02 November 2024

39527922R00073